Look Back

Also by David Hastings

Over the Mountains of the Sea
Extra! Extra! How the people made the news
The Many Deaths of Mary Dobie
Odyssey of the Unknown Anzac
The Vocabulary Detective: How to get meaning from context

Visit David Hastings' author page at Amazon.com
https://www.amazon.com/author/davidhastings01

David Hastings at Goodreads
https://www.goodreads.com/davidhastings01

Look Back

How to talk about the past in English

David Hastings

DMH Press

First published 2023
DMH Press
Auckland
New Zealand
dmhcosmo@outlook.com

ISBN: 9798390749920

Cover design: Micaela Hastings
www.mhastingsdesign.com

Cover image: iStock

Table of Contents

Introduction

History is full of strange, funny and odd events that make entertaining stories: lucky escapes, haunted palaces, wild adventures and great scams as well as kings and queens behaving badly. Their entertainment value makes them ideal texts for people learning English as a second language because reading them should be a pleasure and not seem like so much hard work. Furthermore, as they are all set in past times, they are great for getting acquainted with and practising the various ways you can talk about the past in English.

The twenty stories in this collection are full of examples demonstrating how to understand and use those different ways. But this book is not a formal grammar. It simplifies complex grammatical rules into ten key questions based on the meaning. The grammar comes later. Moreover, rather than deal with one grammatical form at a time, as do most textbooks, it demonstrates them working together. In other words, the text is authentic. In the real world, no one speaks or writes only in the past simple or only in the present perfect, you need to be able to combine the different ways of talking about the past.

Look Back is the second in the *Vocabulary Detective* series, which is aimed at autonomous learners, that is people who want to develop and improve their English language skills independently, outside the classroom. In my opinion, exploring the language in this way – having language adventures as I call them – and taking responsibility for your own progress, is essential to gaining mastery.

At the end of the book on pages 117-139 is a comprehensive guide to the ten questions. They are clearly numbered **(1)** to **(10)** and each one includes an outline of the meaning followed by the grammatical forms that you need to express it. For instance, question **(1)** says "Was it an action at a definite time in the past that was finished?" Then there is an explanation that you will need to use the past simple if that is the meaning you have in mind.

It is only natural that learners will want to go straight to the guide to find out what the ten ways of talking about the past are. But the guide is at the end of the book for a reason. Before you use it, try reading a few of the stories and doing the accompanying exercises which are all based on contrasting the different meanings in the ten questions. In this way you will hopefully develop an understanding of how to talk, think and write about the past in English based on the meaning without getting bogged down in grammatical terminology such as the difference between the past perfect and present perfect.

Each story is followed by two activities. The first is a series of questions in which you choose which of two or more options best matches the meaning of different verbs forms highlighted in the story. By contrasting the options, you will be able to recognise and learn the meaning of each one. For instance, the first question in "Off to a bad start" highlights the verbs **was taken** and **was lying** and asks you to choose which "expresses **(1)** something that happened at a definite time in the past and was finished and which expresses **(3)** something that was still in progress, in other words, unfinished". The contrast in this example, highlights the difference in meaning between the past simple, **(1) was taken**, and the past progressive, **(3) was lying**.

2

The next exercise is designed to take it a step further and start you practising. It consists of a short summary of the story you have just read with five gaps and a selection of five verbs. Your task is to choose which verb fits which gap in the summary. For instance, in the summary of "Off to a bad start", the first sentence reads, "When King Louis XIII **A ...** in 1643, he was succeeded by his son." So, which of these verbs best fits the gap marked **A ...**, **(1) died (2) was (3) was dying (5) had never wanted (7) would**? In the first exercise you are selecting the meaning to fit the verb, in the second you are doing the reverse, choosing the verb to fit the meaning. The first exercise is designed to help you recognise the meaning, the second is to encourage you to use the verb.

As with the previous activity, the options are numbered to match the ten questions at the back of the book. Answers to all the exercises are on pages 140-44 Eventually, you will need to consult the questions to check your understanding, especially where you have made mistakes. But, as noted above, it is better to try to work it out for yourself first. This is the very essence of learning independently. You are much more likely to gain understanding and remember something if you try to work it out for yourself, even if you make mistakes. And this applies as much to vocabulary as to grammar.

All the story titles are common idiomatic expressions in English and the stories themselves illustrate the meaning of these expressions. So they are ideal for practising the skill of working out the meaning of unknown words and phrases from the context. In brief, you do this by searching the surrounding text for clues that will help you discover the meaning. Only when you have tried this, should you look up a dictionary for an answer or to check whether you have guessed correctly. For a more detailed explanation of how this works, see the first book in this series, *The Vocabulary Detective: How to get meaning from context* which is also available on Amazon.

The stories have been graded as between B1 and C1 levels of the Common European Framework using the Text Inspector website and they appear in order from the easiest to the most difficult. Be aware that they contain many examples of past forms, apart from those highlighted in the text for practice. You should be on the lookout for them and use the ten questions independently to test your understanding. The same goes for the vocabulary. Not only are the titles all well-known expressions or phrases, but there are numerous examples of colloquial and idiomatic language throughout the stories.

While reading you should always be thinking about and noticing the context because it is full of clues to meaning, not only of individual words but also of particular grammatical forms. For instance, a verb in the past simple could refer to **(1)**something that happened at a definite time in the past and was finished or **(2)** a state that existed in the past or **(6)** a past habit or something that happened regularly or often in the past or **(8)** speculation about the past. The only way to tell which meaning is intended is to read the context carefully. For instance, if meaning **(6)** is intended, the past simple will usually be accompanied by an adverb of frequency such as **often** or **usually**. If meaning **(8)** is intended the verb will usually be accompanied by qualifiers such as **likely**, **possibly** or **probably**.

For those who prefer a more grammatical approach, there is a grammatical index on pages 149-50 which references the guide and specific examples of particular grammatical forms throughout the book.

Perhaps the main thing, though, is to enjoy the stories and remember that reading, listening and doing exercises are not enough by themselves to learn a language. You need to practise what you learn as well and that means taking every opportunity to write and, even better, to speak.

And finally, here are the ten basic questions used throughout this book. For detailed explanations see pages 117 to 139.

1. Was it an action at a definite time in the past that was finished?

2. Was it a state that existed in the past?

3. Was it something unfinished or still in progress in the past?

4. Was it something at an indefinite time in the past that still affects the present?

5. Was it something in the past that affected something else in the past?

6. Was it a past habit or something that happened regularly or often?

7. Was it still in the future at the time you are talking about?

8. Is it speculation about the past?

9. Was it something hypothetical or unreal in the past?

10. Was it something that someone said in the past?

Off to a bad start (B1)

One day, back in 1643 a five-year-old boy **was taken** to see his father who **was lying** on his death bed in the Chateau de Saint Germain, just outside Paris. It was obvious to everyone, even the boy, that the father did not have long to live.

The old man was asleep, so the boy **did not spend** much time with him. But after he left the room, one of his father's servants asked him if he wanted to be king. It was not a silly question or a joke, because the dying man was Louis XIII of France and so his son was next in line to the throne.

However, the son was horrified at the thought of becoming king. He burst into tears and said no, he did not want the job. He went further still and threatened to drown himself if his father died.

But there was no escaping his fate. As **had been predicted**, his father did die and, at the age of just five, the boy succeeded to the throne. As he was still a child, he could not actually take the reins of power for himself at first. His mother, Anne of Austria, ruled on his behalf as regent.

It was while Anne was ruling France that a series of revolts known as The Fronde, broke out before the boy had even reached his teenage years.

What with young Louis' reluctance to take the throne and the unrest among the people, things had got off to a bad start. The future did not look very bright. The revolts **probably would**

have made him think that his original instinct was the right one. Why would you ever want to be a king and face problems like that?

But in time the revolts subsided and, as Louis XIV, the boy **would go on** to become the most powerful monarch of his age and arguably the greatest king in French history. He **would** make France a leader in fashion, culture and science. His most visible achievement **would** be the majestic palace that he built at Versailles on the outskirts of Paris.

Millions of tourists flock there every year to marvel at the legacy of the man whose career had got off to such a bad start when, as a reluctant boy-king, he faced a dangerous rebellion. But it had ended in style with him being known the world over as the Sun King.

Questions

A. There are two verbs in the first sentence of this story **was taken** and **was lying**. Which expresses **(1)** something that happened at a definite time and was finished and which expresses **(3)** something that was still in progress?

B. The story says the boy **did not spend** much time with his dying father. Does this refer to **(1)** something that happened at a definite time in the past that was finished or **(2)** a state that existed in the past or **(6)** a past habit or something that happened regularly or often or **(8)** speculation about the past?

C. When the story says the father died as **had been predicted**, is the prediction **(1)** something that happened at a definite time in the past and was finished or **(5)** something that happened in the past before something else in the past, namely the death of the king?

D. When the story says the revolts **probably would have made** him think, is this **(1)** something that happened at a definite time in the past and was finished or **(8)** speculation about the past?

E. When the story says the boy **would go on** to become king, **would** make France a fashion leader and **would** build the palace at Versailles, is the verb **would** expressing **(7)** things that were still in the future or **(8)** speculation about the past?

A (1) ...... (3) ...... B ... C ... D ... E ...

Summary

When King Louis XIII of France **A ...** in 1643 he was succeeded by his son, also called Louis, who **B ...** just a child at the time. Young Louis **C ...** to be king, he had said as much while his father **D ...**. But he could not avoid his duty and, despite his original misgivings, as Louis XIV he **E ...** become the greatest king in French history.

(1) died (2) was (3) was dying (5) had never wanted (7)would.

Brushes with death (B1)

Two of the most influential figures of the twentieth century **might have been** killed in the 1930s, long before they played their roles on the stage of global history. The two were Adolf Hitler and Winston Churchill, sworn enemies in the Second World War. But long before they **would** make decisions about the destiny of nations, they were involved in two car accidents that were almost fatal.

Hitler was the first to have a brush with death. In March 1930 he was in his car with a group made up of five men including Otto Wagener who would become a general in the German Army during the Second World War. After the war, Wagner **wrote** his memoirs and described in detail what had happened the day that Hitler almost died.

They **were travelling** from Munich to Berlin. Hitler **was sitting** in the front next to the driver and the others in the back when, at an intersection in Nuremburg, they **noticed** a huge semi-trailer approaching at speed from the right. The truck **rammed** the car with full force, "T-boned" is the expression used for this kind of crash when one vehicle hits another from the side. The force of the impact **was** so powerful that it **pushed** Hitler's car 20 metres across the road. With just a little more force, the truck would have run over the car and flattened it and everyone inside, said Wagener.

For a few moments, Hitler and the others were trapped with the huge truck looming over them. They could not move from the wreckage until the truck, with a loud revving of the engine and the sound of metal scraping against metal, reversed. They were bruised and shaken, and Hitler was the first to speak.

"Is everyone alive?" he said.

When everyone responded with a "yes" Hitler said, "in fact nothing could have happened to us. We still have not completed our task."

He was of course referring to his dream of dominating the world. But he never did complete his task and one man who played a central role in preventing him was Winston Churchill, Prime Minister of Britain during the war.

Strangely, the following year Churchill also had a brush with death when he was knocked down by a car in New York just before Christmas. He was visiting the United States for a lecture tour when it happened. An old friend **had invited** him to drinks one evening at his house on Fifth Avenue. Churchill took a taxi, but he **had forgotten** the address.

"Not to worry," he thought, "I **have been** there before and I'm sure I'll recognise it."

But his previous visit had been a long time ago and it had been during the day. Now, at night, everything seemed different, and he could not recognise the building. He had wasted a lot of time looking for it and was becoming anxious because he did not want to be late. So, he stopped outside Central Park to ask for directions.

It was at this moment that he made a mistake that turned out to be nearly fatal. He began to cross the road but forgot to look both ways and did not notice a taxi coming towards him. The driver, Mario Contasino, hit the brakes. But the road was wet and slippery, and it was too late. The car hit Churchill with full force.

A few weeks later Churchill would write an article about his brush with death in the *Daily Mail*, a London newspaper. In the article Churchill, who had been in the trenches during the First World War, compared the moment that he was knocked down to the moment during the war that a bomb exploded very close to him.

And he explained what went through his mind as he lay on the road, "I have been run over by a motor car in America. All those worries about being late are now swept away. They do not matter anymore. Here is a real catastrophe. Perhaps it is the end."

Many people on the street also thought it was the end. He heard someone scream, "a man has been killed".

But he was not dead and remained conscious. He recalled that he felt the force of the blow to his forehead and on his thighs. Afterwards came a severe pain over his whole body and he worried that he **would** be paralyzed.

The police detained Contasino, but Churchill told them it was all his own fault, the driver was not to blame. Indeed, it was Contasino who drove him to hospital because no one could get an ambulance. Although many people still thought that he might die, his injuries were not fatal. He had two broken ribs, bruises on his right arm, his chest, his legs and cuts to his forehead and his nose.

In a few days he was sitting up in bed, smoking a cigar and giving advice on how to handle the Great Depression, the economic crisis that was worrying the whole world in those days. When the journalists asked him how he was feeling he said, "battered but not shattered". Contasino **went** to the hospital **every day** to ask how he was, and the Churchills invited him to tea at their hotel, the Waldorf Astoria, to show there were no hard feelings.

How would history have been different if these two accidents had been fatal? It is possible that **if Hitler had died**, there **would not have been** a Second World War. Equally, it is possible that, **if Churchill had been killed**, Great Britain **would have** surrendered in 1939. We can never know for sure. These things are just hypotheses, imagining the past to be different with imagined consequences in the past.

Questions

A. The story says Churchill and Hitler **might have been** killed in car crashes in the 1930s. Is this referring to **(1)** things that happened at a definite time in the past and were finished or is it **(8)** speculation about the past?

B. In the early 1930s were the two leaders' decisions about the destiny of nations **(1)** things that were done and finished at definite times in the past or **(7)** things that were still in the future?

C. Did Wagner write his book **(1)** at a definite time in the past and finish it at that time or **(3)** was it something that was still in progress, in other words, unfinished?

D. Look at the verbs in paragraph three: **were travelling**, **was sitting**, **noticed**, **rammed**, **was** and **pushed**. Of these, which **(1)** express things that happened at a definite time in the past and were finished, **(2)** a state that existed in the past and **(3)**things that were still in progress, in other words, unfinished?

E. Were Churchill's invitation and the fact that he forgot his friend's address **(4)** things that happened at an unspecified or indefinite time in the past which still affected him or **(5)** did they happen before something else in the past – his brush with death – which they affected?

F. Was Churchill's previous visit to his friend's house something **(1)** that happened at a definite time in the past and was finished or **(4)** or something that happened at an unspecified or indefinite time in the past but which was part of his general experience and therefore still had some bearing on him?

G. This is a direct quote from Churchill: "I **have been** there before and I'm sure I'll recognise it". Which of these is the correct way to put his words into **(10)** indirect or reported speech:

Churchill **thought** he **has been** there before and **he's** sure he'll recognise it.

OR

Churchill **thought** he **had been** there before and he **was** sure he would recognise it.

H. Churchill thought the accident **would** lead to paralysis. Was this something **(7)** he predicted at the time but, in fact, never happened or **(8)** speculation about the past?

I. The story says Contasino **went** to the hospital **every day**. Was this **(1)** something that happened once at a definite time and was then finished or **(6)** a past habit or something that happened regularly or often in the past?

J. Is the last paragraph referring to **(7)** things that were still in the future or **(9)** things that did not happen in the past, things that were hypothetical, unreal or imaginary with hypothetical past consequences?

A ... **B** ... **C** ... **D** (1) ......, ..., ... (2) ...... (3) ......, ... **E** ... **F** ... **G** .... **H** ... **I** ... **J** ...

Summary

Adolf Hitler and Winston Churchill were lucky they were not killed in separate car accidents in the early 1930s. Hitler was first to have a brush with death when he **A ...** from Munich to Berlin with a group of henchmen. At an intersection in the city of Nuremburg, a large truck **B ...** into the side of his car, pushing it 20 metres across the road and trapping Hitler and the other passengers inside. Eventually, they were freed and, although no one was seriously hurt, the accident **C ...** fatal if the truck had been going a little faster.

Churchill's lucky escape happened in New York city just before Christmas the following year. He was crossing a busy street and forgot to look both ways to check the traffic. He was hit by a car and his injuries were far more serious that those suffered by Hitler and his cronies. He was in such pain as he lay on the road that he thought he **D ...** die. But he survived and a few days later he was sitting up in his hospital bed talking to newspaper reporters.

No one knows for sure how history would have been different if either of these accidents had been fatal. It is possible that, **E ...** Hitler **E ...** , **E ...** a Second World War. And it is possible that, if Churchill had been killed, Britain would have surrendered to Germany in 1939. But these are things that it is impossible to know for sure.

(1) crashed (3) was travelling (7) was going to (8) might have been (9) if ... had been killed ... there would not have been ...

A nice cuppa (B1+)

In May 1662 a Portuguese princess called Catherine of Braganza **arrived** in the English coastal town of Portsmouth, on her way to marry King Charles II and become Queen of England. When she **came** ashore, the first thing she **wanted** was a nice cup of tea.

But there was no tea, which may seem surprising because nowadays the English are known as a nation of tea drinkers. But back then, in the seventeenth century, it was not so. In fact, it was the Portuguese rather than the British who were the great tea drinkers. Catherine **had been brought up** drinking tea, hence her desire for a "nice cuppa" – a colloquial phrase meaning "a good cup of tea" – on the day she arrived in her new county.

At the time, tea was regarded as an exotic luxury in England and people did not drink it very much. For instance, Samuel Pepys (pronounced "Peeps" despite the spelling), a government official who wrote a famous diary about life in 1660s London, recorded drinking tea for the first time just two years before Catherine arrived. Unfortunately, he did not say what he thought of it, but he only mentions it twice more in the next nine years, so clearly, he wasn't very keen on it.

But was that because of the taste or because of the price? Tea was not only exotic but very, very expensive. It **has been reported** that the price was £2 per pound in 1658 which would be about US$750 per kilogram in 2020 according to the retail price index on measuringworth.com. No wonder tea was not very popular. Ordinary people **used to** drink ale and coffee, two drinks that Pepys mentions frequently.

In the light of this evidence, it is not surprising that when Catherine arrived at Portsmouth, the townsfolk had no tea to offer her and instead **offered** her a glass of ale. But the ale made her feel sick and she had to go and lie down for a little while to recover.

Catherine **went on to** marry King Charles as planned, and the marriage cemented a close alliance between England and Portugal. She **would** also exercise great influence over the King himself, persuading him to convert to the Catholic religion just before he **died**.

But her greatest legacy was tea. She made it the drink of choice at the royal court and from there it became fashionable among the aristocracy. It would take quite a long while, but eventually tea became a drink of the people and, by the the time the eighteenth century was over, England **had changed** from a nation of coffee and ale drinkers into a nation of tea drinkers.

However, while tea drinking **has increased** in England since Catherine's day, it **has decreased** in Portugal. According to a 2016 survey by Statista, a German marketing company, British people consume 1.5kg of tea per capita every year. That makes them fourth in the world. The Portuguese, on the other hand, are 47th, consuming just 0.064kg per capita every year.

So, if Catherine **had arrived** in 2016 instead of 1662, she **would have been** given a nice cuppa instead of an ale. But, then again, if she **had arrived** in 2016, she probably **would have asked** for a cup of coffee.

Questions

A. The first paragraph uses three verbs: **arrived**, **came** and **wanted**. Which two of these verbs **(1)** express things that happened at a definite time in the past and were finished and which one expresses **(2)** a state that existed in the past?

B. Catherine **had been brought up** as a tea drinker. Was this **(1)** something that happened at a definite time in the past and was finished or **(5)** something that happened before something else in the past, namely her arrival in England?

C. Was the information about the price of tea in 1658 something **(1)** that was reported at a definite time in the past and was finished or **(4)** something that was reported at some unspecified or indefinite time in the past?

D. The story says that in the seventeenth century, ordinary people in Britain **used to** drink ale and coffee. Was this **(1)** a state that existed at a definite time in the past and was then finished or **(6)** something that happened regularly or often in the past?

E. Was the offer of a glass of ale to Catherine **(1)** something that happened at a definite time in the past and was finished or **(6)** a past habit or something that happened regularly or often in the past?

F. Catherine **went on to** marry Charles and **would** have a great influence on him. Were these **(1)** things that happened at a definite time in the past and were finished or **(7)** things that, in 1662, were still in the future?

G. The story says King Charles converted to the Catholic faith just before he **died**. Does the verb **died** in this sentence indicate **(1)** something that happened at a definite time in the past and was finished or **(3)** does it indicate something that was still in progress, in other words, unfinished?

19

H. By the end of the eighteenth century, England **had changed** into a nation of tea drinkers. Was this **(1)** something that happened at a definite time in the past and was finished or **(5)** something that happened before something else in the past, the turn of the eighteenth century?

I. Were the rise in tea-drinking in England and the decline in Portugal **(1)** things that happened at a definite time in the past and were finished or **(4)** things that continued for a period after the time of Catherine and still affect the present?

J. In the last paragraph, the story makes two comments about 2016. Were these **(1)** things that happened at a definite time in the past and were finished or **(9)** things that did not happen in the past, they were unreal, hypothetical or imaginary with hypothetical consequences in the past?

A (1) ......, ... **(2)** ...... **B** ... **C** ... **D** ... **E** ... **F** ... **G** ... **H** ... **I** ... **J** ...

Summary

Catherine of Braganza **A** ... a Portuguese princess who **B** ... King Charles II of England in the seventeenth century. She was highly influential at the royal court in London but her greatest claim to fame **C** ... that she taught the English how to drink tea. Before Catherine, the English didn't use to drink tea, they preferred coffee or ale. But Catherine **D** ... tea in her native Portugal and she kept up the habit in England. Soon drinking tea became fashionable at court. In one of history's ironies, England **E** ... a nation of tea drinkers since Catherine's day while Portugal has become a nation of coffee drinkers.

(1) married (2) was (4) has become (6) drank (8) may have been

A formidable woman (B1+)

Shortly before the Second World War **broke out**, Hermione Llewellyn **married** the love of her life, Daniel Knox. When she **did** this, she not only **became** a married woman but also a countess because Knox was the sixth Count of Ranfurly. So, from then on, she was known as Lady Ranfurly on formal occasions.

The two were very happy and they loved to spend their leisure time in aristocratic sports such as horse riding and hunting deer in the Highlands of Scotland. In fact, they **were hunting** in the Highlands when the war **began**.

They **were staying** with an old friend who **was** usually very happy and hospitable. But one evening, after a day in the mountains, they returned to the house to find their host in a bad mood. At first, they were worried and thought he must have been offended by something that they had done.

But no, the cause of his bad humour was the news that Germany had invaded Poland and the war that everyone dreaded, had begun. As Dan, or Lord Ranfurly, was an officer in the British Army reserve, the happy couple had to return to London immediately.

A few weeks later Dan was preparing to go to the Middle East. He would be stationed in the land that is now called Israel but in those days was known as Palestine and the newly married couple would have to separate after just a short time together.

In those days the wives of regular army officers were allowed to accompany their husbands on overseas postings but the wives of reserve officers, like Dan, had to stay behind.

But Hermione, Lady Ranfurly, had not the slightest doubt that her role was at the side of her husband. What's more, she was a strong personality and was not about to give up. On the contrary, she was always up for a challenge. Indeed, you could say she was a formidable women, meaning a tough, strong or forceful woman.

As soon as her husband had gone, she began to investigate how she could follow him. Someone introduced her to a travel agent who organised her trip. She **would** travel by train to Marseilles and there she **would** embark on a ship which **would** take her across the Mediterranean to Egypt or Palestine.

During the voyage she wrote in her diary "I am lovesick, homesick … and now seasick."

Despite all this, and not for the last time, Hermione got her own way and was reunited with Dan in Palestine. At first everything went very well. Hermione and a good friend, Toby, who was also married to a reserve officer, found a couple of humble cottages to rent and set about looking for work. They applied for jobs as secretaries because there were many organizations who needed English speakers to do this kind of work.

Many employers were surprised that a countess had the skills of a stenographer, but she **had learned** how to do this when she **had worked** as an adviser to the governor of New South Wales in Australia during the 1930s. In fact, it was there that she met Dan who was also on the staff at Government House in Sydney.

So, she found work with the Red Crescent, equivalent to the Red Cross in the Middle East. **At weekends** or **whenever** Dan had free time from the Army, they **got together** and were as happy as possible, given the circumstances.

The top generals of the Army called Hermione and the other wives of reserve officers "the illegals" and sent them back to England on a big ocean liner called the *British Empire*. All the women on board accepted their fate, except Hermione who jumped ship – an expression which means left the ship illegally – at Cape Town in South Africa. She flew from South Africa to Egypt on a flying boat and had to hide from the authorities in Cairo who **would have been** furious **if they had known** what she had done.

Eventually they did realise that Hermione had returned and the generals again tried to send her back to England. But by this time, she had succeeded in finding work with the government and was able to stay.

She was feeling very pleased with herself but a few weeks later she heard news that the *British Empire* **had been** bombed in the Atlantic Ocean off the coast of Ireland. The ship had caught fire and had sunk although most of the passengers and crew **had been** saved. Hermione was worried about her friend Toby and when news came a few days later, it was not good. Unfortunately, Toby was one of the unlucky ones although no one was sure about exactly what **had happened** to her. One report said she **had been** reading a book in the lounge when a bomb crashed through the ceiling and started a fire.

It was a lucky escape for Hermione, but she had her own share of bad luck later when her husband was captured in the North African desert. They would be reunited at the end of the war but, in the meantime, Hermione remained in the Middle East doing what she could to help the war effort. There were no more attempts to send her home. One of the generals made the surrender official when he wrote that she had defeated all the generals in the Middle East and he was not **going to go** into battle against such a formidable young woman.

Questions

A. The first sentence of this story has four verbs – **broke out**, **married**, **did** and **became** – do they refer to **(1)** things that happened at definite times and were finished or **(2)** states that existed in the past and no longer exist or **(3)** things that were still in progress, in other words, unfinished?

B. Look at the verbs **were hunting** and **began** in the second paragraph. Which one refers to **(1)** something that happened at a definite time in the past and was finished and which one refers to **(3)** something that was still in progress, in other words, unfinished?

C. Look at the verbs **were staying** and **was** in the third paragraph. Which one refers to **(2)** a state that existed in the past and was finished and which one refers to **(3)** something that was still in progress, in other words, unfinished?

D. The story gives an outline of Hermione's trip from Britain to the Middle East using the verb **would**: she **would** travel, she **would** embark and the ship **would** take her. Does the verb **would** in this context refer to **(6)** a past habit or something that happened regularly or often in the past or **(7)** things that were still in the future?

E. The story quotes Hermione as saying, "I am lovesick, homesick … and now seasick". Which of these is the correct way to put her words in **(10)** indirect speech:

Hermione **said** I **am** lovesick, homesick … and now seasick.
OR
Hermione **said** she **was** lovesick, homesick … and now seasick?

F. The story says Hermione **had learned** how to be a stenographer when she **had worked** in Australia. Did she **(1)** do these things at a definite time in the past and finish them or did she **(5)** do them before something else in the past, her jobs in the Middle East during the Second World War?

G. The story uses the past simple in the phrase **got together** to talk about Dan and Hermione meeting each other **at weekends** during the war and **whenever** Dan had free time. Does this mean that it was something that **(1)** they did at a definite time in the past and was finished or **(6)** was it a past habit or something that happened regularly or often in the past?

H. The story says the generals **would have been** furious with Hermione **if they had known** she had returned to Cairo. Is this **(1)** something that happened at a definite time in the past and was finished or **(9)** something that did not happen, in other words was just hypothetical, unreal or imaginary with hypothetical consequences in the past?

I. The second last paragraph describes the sinking of the *British Empire*. It says the ship **had been** bombed, most of the passengers **had been** saved, no one knew what **had happened** to Toby, but she **had been** reading a book when the ship was attacked. Were these **(1)** things that happened at a definite time in the past and were finished or **(5)** things that happened before other things in the past?

J. The final paragraph paraphrases the general who was not **going to go** into battle against Hermione. Was he referring to **(3)** something that was still in progress, in other words, unfinished or **(7)** was he talking about the future?

A … B (1) …… (3) …… C (2) …… (3) …… D …
E…………………………………………………………………
…. F … G … H … I … J …

Summary

Hermione Ranfurly was an English countess who **A** ... when the Second World War began. She and her husband, Dan, **B** ... in the Scottish Highlands at the time but their carefree life was about to be disrupted. Dan was in the army and when he was sent to the Middle East, she followed him even though military regulations said this was not allowed. In her diary she wrote that, on the ship going there, she **C** ... homesick, lovesick and seasick. Unfortunately for Hermione, the generals in the Middle East decided she had to go home and she was sent back, with many other military wives, on a ship called the *British Empire*. Unlike the others, she **D** ... to accept her fate. She jumped ship in Cape Town and flew back to Cairo to be reunited with her husband. It turned out to be a lucky escape because the *British Empire* **E** ... be bombed and sunk in the Atlantic Ocean before it reached its destination and one of her best friends would be killed.

(1) refused (3) were hunting (5) had just got married (7)would (10) was

First impressions (B1+)

In 1877 Paris, a struggling artist by the name of Camille Pissarro **was** so desperate to create interest in his paintings that he **decided** to raffle one. He was part of an emerging school of artists known as the Impressionists who **were getting** a hard time from the critics.

One described them as "six madmen and a mad woman" and their works **were routinely rejected** for inclusion in the most important exhibitions.

The general opinion of their work was so low that you could pick up a painting by Claude Monet for as little as 35 francs and Pissarro's paintings **were** even cheaper at seven or ten francs apiece.

Then Pissarro **held** his raffle but it **did not solve** the problem. A little girl **was** the winner and unfortunately, she **shared** the opinion of the art critics and **rejected** the painting and **asked** for a cream bun instead.

It is not known whether she ever lived to realise her mistake or, indeed, whether the Parisian art critics ever regretted pouring scorn on the Impressionists. But the Impressionist painters eventually became admired as among the greatest artists in all history and today their works fetch prices that match their reputation.

For instance, a Pissarro painting titled "Boulevard Montmartre, Spring Morning" **sold** at auction for US$32 million in 2014. Works of other Impressionists can fetch far more. Four years later a Monet titled "Meules" (Haystacks) **went for** US$110.7 million.

It just goes to show that there is a lot of truth in the old saying, first impressions are not always best.

Questions

A. Look at the verbs **was**, **decided** and **were getting** in the first paragraph. Which one refers to **(1)** something that happened at a particular time in the past and was finished, which one refers to **(2)** a state that existed in the past and which one refers to **(3)** things that were still in progress, in other words, unfinished?

B. Was the rejection of the works of the Impressionists by art galleries in the 1870s **(1)** something that happened once at a definite time in the past and was finished or was it **(6)** a past habit or something that happened regularly or often in the past?

C. Paragraph three says Pisarro's paintings **were** even cheaper than Monet's. Was this **(1)** something that happened at a particular time in the past and was finished or **(2)** was it a state that existed in the past?

D. Look at the six verbs in paragraph four – **held**, **did not solve**, **was, shared**, **rejected** and **asked** – which refer to things that **(1)** happened or were done at a definite time in the past and were finished and which refer to **(2)** states that existed for a time in the past?

E. In the final paragraph do the verbs **sold** and **went for** mean **(1)** things that happened at a definite time in the past and were finished or **(3)** things that were still in progress, in other words, unfinished?

A (1) ...... **(2)** ...... **(3)** ...... **B** ... **C** ... **D (1)** ......, ..., ..., ... **(2)** ......, ... **E** ...

Summary

Camille Pissarro, a struggling artist in Paris, **A** ... to raffle one of his paintings in 1877 in the hope of creating some interest in his work which **B** ... harshly judged by the city's art critics. A little girl won the raffle but unfortunately for Pissarro, she shared the critics' opinion and, instead of the painting, she asked if could have a cream bun. But, in the end, the joke was on her and the critics. Pissarro **C** ... a member of the Impressionist school of painting. In time they **D** ... become famous and their paintings would sell for millions of dollars. The critics and the child probably **E** ... themselves if they had known.

(1) decided (2) was (3) was being (7) would (8) would have kicked

The last laugh (B2)

History is full of stories about great kings fighting it out for supremacy on the battlefield. Stories about kings trying to outdo each other in the field of fashion are not so common but one such contest **took place** in the late seventeenth century when Charles II was king of England and his opposite number in France was Louis XIV.

During Louis' reign France **became** the leader of all things cultural in Europe, including fashion. Everyone at the English court of Charles followed the French style of Louis' Versailles. What's more, there was much admiration for the way that Louis conducted himself as king. The famous diarist of 1660s London, Samuel Pepys, recorded how he had once attended a dinner party where the guests greatly praised Louis for the way he **had raised** his kingdom and himself to greatness.

As Charles' biographer, Antonia Fraser remarks, Charles **would have been** less than human **if he had not been affected** by such talk. No one likes being overshadowed, least of all a king with his own dreams of greatness. This was the background to what became known as the "Persian Vest" incident in which Charles tried to free himself and his court from the tyranny of French fashion.

Although Charles started the duel, he did it from a position of weakness because he had never been much interested in fashion. He had no sense of style. Nevertheless, he **designed** an outfit which was loosely described as a vest and resembled paintings of the styles worn at the Persian court. Pepys describe the garment as being worn under a coat and over a white, silk shirt. Pretty soon everyone at court **was wearing** one of the "Persian vests". It seemed like the English court had well and truly broken free of French fashion.

But if Charles started the duel, it was Louis who finished it. Within a few weeks news drifted back over the English Channel that Louis had pulled off a right royal piece of one-upmanship when he **ordered** the servants at Versailles to dress in the style of the English aristocracy. And the French aristocracy **were telling** their servants to do likewise.

When Pepys **heard** the news at dinner one night, he **felt** mixed emotions. On the one hand he was outraged by the insult which he described as the "greatest indignity ever done by one Prince to another". It made King Charles seem small and insignificant and he sincerely hoped Charles would get his revenge somehow. And yet it made him laugh as well because it was such an ingenious example of one-upmanship, Louis had certainly got the better of Charles.

Indeed, it was so ingenious that there really was no way of getting revenge at the time. Pretty soon French fashion was once again supreme in the English court. But there **has been** a kind of revenge in posterity, in the end it was Charles who had the last laugh even though it was posthumous.

The fashion of Louis XIV is now a thing of the past but the modern waistcoat, which is worn underneath a jacket and over a shirt just like the one in the 1660s, is said to be a direct descendent of the Persian vests of Charles II. What's more, in the United States and Australia, they still call it a vest thus proving the wisdom of the old saying "he who laughs last, laughs longest". However, sometime people say, "laughs best" or "laughs loudest" instead of "longest".

Questions

A. The introduction says a contest over fashion **took place** between the kings of France and England in the seventeenth century. Was this **(1)** something that happened at a definite time in the past and was finished or **(3)** was it something that was still in progress, in other words, unfinished?

B. Was the fact that France **became** the cultural leader of Europe **(1)** something that happened at a definite time in the past and was finished or **(3)** something that was still in progress, in other words, unfinished?

C. Was the fact that Louis **had raised** his kingdom to greatness **(1)** something that happened at a definite time in the past and was finished or **(5)** something that happened before something else in the past – the dinner party?

D. Look at this sentence: "Charles **would have been** less than human **if he had not been affected**". Is this **(8)** speculation about the past or **(9)** something that did not happen, in other words something unreal, hypothetical or imaginary with hypothetical past consequences?

E. Was Charles' design for the Persian vest something **(1)** that happened at a definite time in the past and was finished or **(3)** was it still in progress, in other words, unfinished?

F. The story says everyone at court **was wearing** the Persian vests. Was this something **(1)** that happened at a definite time in the past and was finished or **(3)** was it still in progress, in other words, unfinished?

G. Louis **ordered** the servants at Versailles to dress in the English style. Was this something **(1)** that he did at a definite time in the past and was finished or **(3)** was it still in progress, in other words, unfinished?

H. The story says the French aristocracy **were telling** their servants to do the same. Was this **(1)** something that happened at a definite time in the past and was finished or **(3)** was it still in progress, in other words, unfinished?

I. The story describes how Pepys **heard** the news and how he **felt**. Which of these verbs **(1)** expressed something that happened at a definite time in the past and was finished and which **(2)** expresses a state that existed in the past?

J. Is the statement that there **has been** a kind of revenge, referring to **(1)** something that happened at a definite time in the past and is now finished or **(4)** did it happen at some unspecified or indefinite time in the past but which, in some way, still affects the present?

A ... B ... C ... D ... E ... F ... G ... H ... I (1) ...... (2)...... J ...

Summary

In the 1660s all the lords and ladies at the court of King Charles II in London **A ...** in the French style. Then as now, France **B ...** very much the leader fashion. But Charles wanted to break away from French influence and assert his own independence so, even though he **C ...** interested in fashion, he **D ...** to create an English style. He did this by designing a vest or waistcoat based on pictures he had seen of the Persian court. Soon all the aristocrats at his court **E ...** these "Persian vests" which were made of silk. But then Charles' great rival, Louis XIV of France heard about it. Determined to maintain France's position as the fashion leader of Europe, he ordered that all the servants at the Palace of Versailles should be dressed in the English aristocratic style. Soon all servants of the wealthy and noble houses of Europe were dressed like English aristocrats and Louis had proved himself to be a master of one-upmanship, that is, gaining an advantage over other people.

(1) decided (2) Was (3) were wearing (5) had never been (6) dressed

Prophet of doom (B2)

Towards the end of the eighteenth century and the beginnings of the nineteenth, there **were** many social, political and religious disputes and conflicts in Europe and North America. It was the era of the French Revolution, the war of independence in the United States and other major conflicts on the continent of Europe.

Of course, lots of people were worried about all of this. In England, the government and members of Parliament were worried that the masses might follow the example of the French and rise up in revolution. At the same time, many among the masses **had lost** confidence in their political and religious leaders and **were looking** for alternative sources of guidance.

In response, some individuals declared themselves to be prophets and claimed to have all the answers to the uncertainties of the age. One of the most famous of them in the 1790s was Richard Brothers who assured his followers that he was in direct contact with God, and the Almighty not only spoke to him but listened to him as well.

Brothers was a prophet of doom, that is a religious figure who predicted disasters ahead. By the 1790s, he had attracted many followers and one day he prophesied that, at a specific time in January 1791, the city of London **was going to be** destroyed as a punishment for the many sins of Londoners. He knew this, he said, because God had told him personally. So powerful were his words, and such was their impact, that thousands of people immediately fled the city in pure terror.

At exactly the time that Brothers had prophesied, a great storm broke over London. An Irish journalist, John Binns, was walking down The Strand on his way to a meeting at the time and he described the moment. It was evening when the storm began with a powerful wind, then the heavy rain swept in, bringing with it great flashes of lightning and the menacing rumble of thunder drawing ever closer.

Binns **sought** shelter in the nearest pub where he found fifty or sixty people who **had done** the same. There were men, women and children and it seemed to Binns that they knew what the prophet had said and most of them believed the world was about to end.

Many years later, in his autobiography, Binns **would** record what happened at that fateful moment. It was a very strange scene. Most of the people were in a state of alarm or panic. Some **were praying** to God and begging for mercy. But it seemed to Binns that others did not believe the prophecy, nor did they believe in God. They **did not stop drinking** beer and **were laughing** at the fearful ones who **were praying**.

Binns would say that never in his life before that moment had he witnessed such a ferocious storm. But it was all over in fifteen or twenty minutes. London wasn't destroyed, the world didn't end and no one died.

Of course, this was great news for the people who had been so fearful because of the prophecy. But you would think that it **would have been** a disaster for the prophet, a major credibility crisis. As he had told everyone that God had told him personally that London would be destroyed, the failure of the prediction was surely proof that he was not in contact with the Almighty at all. **If he had really known** God's intentions, he **would not have been** mistaken in this way.

But Brothers had an ingenious answer to this problem.

"I **prayed** to God and asked him to give you sinners another chance," he said. And he went on to describe how God **had lifted** him up to the heavens and they **had discussed** the matter while seated on two clouds.

"As a result of these negotiations," said Brothers, "God has agreed to give you one more chance to behave yourselves."

"But, be warned," he said, "Only one more chance. The last chance. From now on you have to be more moral, more ethical and more honest. Or else!"

And once again the people believed the prophet. And so, instead of becoming known as a false prophet on the strength of his failed prediction, Brothers became even more famous and powerful and attracted even more followers.

But that was not the end of the story because a few years later he made another incorrect prediction which got him into serious trouble. He predicted that King George III would die in 1795 and the British monarchy would end. When these things did not happen, Brothers was charged with treason and was imprisoned for being criminally insane. He spent the next ten years behind bars before being released into the care of a friend. He died in 1824.

The phrase "prophet of doom" is still in use though it applies to anyone who has a consistently pessimistic or gloomy outlook, not necessarily based on religion.

Questions

A. Did the many social, political and religious disputes and conflicts **(1)** happen at a definite time in the past and were finished or **(2)** were they states that existed in the past?

B. The verbs **had lost** and **were looking** appear in the second paragraph. Which one **(3)** expresses something that was still in progress, in other words, unfinished, and which one **(5)** expresses something that happened in the past before something else in the past?

C. When Brothers said London **was going to be** destroyed was he **(1)** referring to something that happened at a definite time in the past and was finished or **(7)** was he predicting something, in other words talking about the future?

D. Look at this sentence from the story: "Binns **sought** shelter in the nearest pub where he found fifty or sixty people who **had done** the same". Which verb **(1)** describes something that happened at a particular time in the past and was finished and which **(5)** describes something that happened before something else in the past?

E. Look at this sentence: "Many years later, in his autobiography, Binns **would** record what happened". Does the verb **would** in this context mean **(6)** a past habit or something that happened regularly or often in the past or **(7)** was it something that was still in the future?

F. Several verbs are used to describe what people were doing in the pub when Binns entered – **were praying**, **did not stop drinking** and **were laughing** – were these **(1)** things that happened at a definite time and were finished or were they **(3)** things that were still in progress, in other words, unfinished?

G. Look at this sentence: "But you would think that it **would have been** a disaster for the prophet". Does **would have been** express (7) something that was still in the future or (9) something that did not happen, something hypothetical, unreal or imaginary?

H. Look at this sentence: "**If he had really known** God's intentions, he **would not have been** mistaken in this way". Does this pattern express **(6)** a past habit or something that happened regularly or often or **(7)** something was still in the future in the 1790s or **(8)** speculation about the past or **(9)** something that did not happen, something hypothetical, unreal or imaginary with hypothetical past consequences?

I. When Brothers said "I **prayed** to God" was he **(1)** expressing something that happened at a definite time in the past and was finished or **(3)** something that was still in progress, in other words, unfinished?

J. He described how God **had lifted** him up to the heavens and they **had discussed** the matter. Were these **(1)** things that happened at a definite time in the past and were finished or **(10)** were they indirect speech for his actual words which were "God **lifted** me up to the heavens and we **discussed** the matter".

A ... B (3) ...... (5) ...... C ... D (1) ...... (5) ...... E ... F... G ... H ... I ... J ...

Summary

Richard Brothers predicted that London **A ...** be destroyed in January 1791 because the people **B ...** so sinful. He said he knew this because God himself had told him. Sure enough, on the given day, the city was hit by a furious thunderstorm. There was thunder and lightning and it **C ...** heavily. Some said it was the wildest thunderstorm they **D ....** It seemed that the prophecy was about to come true. But then the storm blew over. This **E...** the end of Brothers' credibility and his career as a prophet but for one thing. He told everyone that he had personally spoken to God and asked him to give the people one more chance to behave themselves and, luckily, God had agreed. And so the disaster was averted and, instead losing his credibility, Brothers became more popular than ever.

(2) were (3) was raining (4) had ever experienced (7) was going to (9) would have been

Tragedy plus time (B2)

It is often said that the definition of comedy or humour is "tragedy plus time". The quotation **has been attributed to** the famous nineteenth-century novelist Mark Twain and the twentieth-century comedians Steve Allen and Lenny Bruce. The best we can say is that each one **may have expressed** the basic idea at some time. What's more, it's an idea that predates all of them. The great political philosopher, Thomas Hobbes, wrote something similar back in the seventeenth century although he did not put it quite as crisply as humour being "tragedy plus time".

A classic example to illustrate the meaning of the quotation is a scene in the famous British comedy film *Monty Python and the Holy Grail*. The scene is set in a time of plague, not unlike the Black Death which killed millions of people in Europe and North Africa in the fourteenth century or the Great Plague that devastated London during the seventeenth century, the latter occurring not long after Hobbes made his observation about things that are tragic at the time they happen, can seem funny later. Thousands and thousands of people **were dying**, and some people **were appointed** as body collectors to go through the streets **at night** to collect corpses which they **carried** on "dead carts" to a place of mass burials near the River Thames.

They **used to** signal their presence by calling out, "Bring out your dead! Bring out your dead!" The plague was a tragedy on a grand scale and no one **would have** dreamed of making a joke out of it at the time. Yet the Monty Python comedy troupe did just that hundreds of years later. The scene shows an old man being carried to the dead cart by his son. "But I'm not dead yet," cries the old man.

"Yes he is … well, he will be soon, he's very ill," says the son to the body collector, who, after some hesitation, hits the old man over the head to fulfill the son's prophecy.

The film was a huge success in the English-speaking world and while there were doubtless some people who found the scene tasteless, most people laughed along with it. Obviously, Londoners back in the 1660s or those who lived at the time of the Black Death would not have found it at all funny. The difference is, of course, the time, the hundreds years between those plagues and when the film was made. That was what enabled the comedians to make a joke out of a tragic set of circumstances.

If they had done a little more research, they **might have found** a true story in the plague of London that was just as funny as the one they invented and similarly, no joke at the time that it happened. It began with a scene very much like the one depicted in *Monty Python and the Holy Grail*, the dead cart going through the streets of London with the body collectors' crying, "Bring out your dead! Bring out your dead!"

At some point they came across a man lying dead in the street. By his side was a set of bagpipes. These famous musical instruments come from Scotland and if played well they are hauntingly beautiful but if played badly they sound like a couple of tomcats fighting in the early hours of the morning. The body collectors, rightly assuming that the bagpipes belonged to the dead man, threw them on the cart with the corpse.

But in the memoirs of a British MP, Sir John Reresby, the piper was not dead at all, but drunk. In fact, you could say that he was "dead drunk" which is not to say "dead" but rather "extremely drunk". Reresby, who swore that the story was true, said the man **had fallen over** in the street and was fast asleep when the body collectors gathered him up.

He **remained** on the cart all night but in the grey misty morning, just as they were nearing their destination, he woke up and decided to greet the dawn with a tune on his pipes. The body collectors were scared out of their wits to see and hear what looked like a phantom rise from the pile of corpses, accompanied by the music of the bagpipes. Unfortunately, Reresby does not tell us whether the man played well or badly but either way it didn't matter much to the body collectors. They took to their heels and ran, convinced that they had been carrying the devil around on their cart all night disguised as a dead man.

If you find the story funny, remove the 350-year time gap and imagine yourself as one of the body collectors. **If that had happened** to you, **would you have laughed**?

Questions

A. Does the verb form **has been attributed to** in the introduction refer to **(1)** something that happened at a definite time in the past and was finished or **(4)** was it something that happened at some unspecified or indefinite time in the past which forms part of general experience and therefore has some bearing on the present?

B. When the story says Twain, Allen and Bruce "**may have expressed** the basic idea" is this **(1)** something that happened at a particular time in the past and was finished or **(8)** speculation about the past?

C. The story says thousands of people **were dying** during the plague and some people **were appointed** as body collectors. Which of those verbs expressed **(1)** things that happened at a definite time in the past and were finished and **(3)** something that was still in progress, in other words, unfinished?

D. The body collectors **carried** the corpses to mass burial sites **at night**. The verb **carried** is in the past simple but is it expressing **(1)** something that happened at a definite time in the past and was finished or is it **(2)** a state that existed in the past or **(6)** a past habit or something that happened regularly or often in the past or **(8)** speculation about the past?

E. They **used to** call "bring out your dead". Was this something **(1)** that happened at a definite time in the past and was finished or **(6)** a past habit or something that happened regularly or often in the past?

F. The story says no one at the time of the plague **would have** dreamed of making a joke out of it. Is this **(1)** something that happened at a definite time in the past and was finished or is it **(8)** speculation about the past?

G. Look at this sentence: "**If they had done** a little more research, they **might have found** a true story". Is it referring to **(5)** something that happened before something else in the past or **(9)** to something that did not happen, in other words something unreal, hypothetical or imaginary with hypothetical past consequences?

H. Sir John Reresby said that man **had fallen over** in the street. Was he referring to **(2)** a state that existed in the past or is this **(10)** indirect speech for what he actually said: "the bagpiper … **fell over** …"

I. When the story says the bagpiper **remained** on the cart, does it mean **(1)** something that happened at a definite time in the past and was finished or **(6)** a past habit or something that happened regularly or often in the past?

J. The story ends with a question: "**If that had happened** to you, **would you have laughed**?" Is the question about **(1)** something that happened at a definite time in the past and is now finished or **(9)** about something that did not happen, something unreal, hypothetical or imaginary with hypothetical past consequences?

A ... B ... C **(1)** ...... **(3)** ...... D ... E ... F ... G ... H ... I ... J ...

Summary

The Great Plague of London in 1665 was so bad that it killed 100,000 people, about a quarter of the city's population. The bodies of those who died were collected at night by teams of men who **A** ...... go through the streets calling "bring out your dead, bring out your dead". The bodies **B** ...... on carts and taken to mass graves for burial in the morning. One night, they **C** ... a man lying on the road next to a set of bagpipes. Assuming him to be another victim of the plague, they threw him on their cart with the other bodies and carried on their work. But the man was not dead. He was drunk and when they **D** ... ready to dump the bodies, he woke up and started to play a tune on his bagpipes. The carters were terrified. They thought they **E** ... carrying the devil around all night and they took to their heels and ran.

(1) found (3) were getting (5) had been (6) would (6) were loaded

Too good to be true (B2)

Whenever Charles Ponzi **spoke**, people **paid** attention. Ponzi, who founded the Securities Exchange Company in Boston in 1920, was known as a financial wizard because he claimed to have found the secret to making a fortune. He was a small man with a loud voice and plenty of charisma. But it was not just these qualities that commanded attention. It was what he said. He promised his investors that they **would** double their money in 90 days or, if they were more cautious, he **would** pay them 50 per cent interest for 45 days.

It seemed too good to be true, and soon crowds **were gathering** outside the small office of his company in School Street for fear of missing out on a great opportunity to get rich quick. They came in their thousands, some people with just a few dollars and others with their life savings. Still others **would** mortgage their houses so they could share in the promise of easy money.

As well as the huge returns he was offering, Ponzi's powerful sense of self-confidence was of vital importance in persuading so many people to trust him. But what **must have been** even more important, was the fact that he **was prepared** to share his secret with the public. He told them he **had discovered** a way of making a fortune by trading in international postal coupons. In the early twentieth century, these coupons **were** used for reply-paid mail. That is, when someone, usually a company, sent correspondence internationally they **would** include the cost of the postage for the reply in the form of a coupon. The coupons could be bought in about sixty countries and Ponzi told everyone that he was exploiting the difference between weak currencies and strong ones to make money. For example, he would buy the coupons cheap in a country with a weak currency, say Italy, and sell them at a higher price in country with a strong currency, for instance the United States.

In a few short months in 1920 he went from being almost penniless to a multi-millionaire as people rushed to invest in his scheme. The figure most frequently cited was $15 million. Nowadays, according to measuringworth.com, the amount he raised would be worth $3.5 billion, calculated as a share of the gross domestic product of the United States.

Everything **was going** very well for Ponzi, until the authorities and the *Boston Post* newspaper **began** investigating. Because of these investigations, Ponzi had to stop accepting new investments and this started a panic. School Street was still full of people but now the crowds were not there to deposit their money but to withdraw it as soon as possible.

Despite the panic, Ponzi continued to express confidence and he kept up appearances throughout the crisis. He said the authorities didn't understand anything about his company's business and he would continue to pay his debts and settle his obligations without any problems at all. He boasted about his success and told the journalists who sought him out for comment every day that one of the banking officials had declined an offer to invest in his company. If he had done so, said Ponzi, he would have made $5000 in 45 days. It seemed that Ponzi's confidence had no limits. *The New York Times* reported that he had plans to create a new banking system and to make Boston the biggest import and export hub in the United States.

Although Ponzi was always saying that he could cover his debts, this was the beginning of the end for his scheme. Unfortunately for the investors, Ponzi was operating a type of fraud or scam which, in those days, **was known** as "robbing Peter to pay Paul". People who operated scams like this did, as Ponzi did, and offered impossibly high rates of interest. In effect, they created an illusion which sucked in customers. To maintain the illusion, the scamsters used money from their new investors (Peter) to pay the interest to the previous investors (Paul). In this way the scheme can grow very quickly and keep growing until it runs out of new investors. With no more new money to pay the interest to the old investors and maintain the illusion, the scam suddenly collapses and almost everyone loses.

This is what happened to the Securities Exchange Company when it stopped taking new investors at the very moment that the old investors were demanding their money back. Ponzi's victims lost 70 per cent of their money and Ponzi himself was sent to jail for fraud.

In the aftermath of the scandal, it became clear that Ponzi's scheme for making money out of postal coupons was impossible for two reasons. First it **was not** possible to convert the coupons to cash, as Ponzi claimed, they **could be used** only to buy stamps. Second, and even more important, the face value of all the postal coupons in the world was nowhere near the amount of money that Ponzi was talking about. US postal officials would say that in the six years before Ponzi launched his scam, the value of all the coupons in the world had been $500,000 but Ponzi was claiming that the value of his investment scheme was $15 million. So, even if Ponzi **had been**

able to control the whole market in coupons and stamps, he **could not have** earned money in sufficient quantities to sustain his business.

Such was Ponzi's impact that the old "robbing Peter to pay Paul" scam is now known as a "Ponzi Scheme" even though he did not actually invent it himself. There are many examples of Ponzi schemes in history. The most infamous of the twenty-first century was that of Bernie Madoff in New York which collapsed after the global financial crisis of 2008. Using the Ponzi method, Madoff swindled or conned his victims to the tune of $19 billion.

As for Ponzi himself, after he had served his time, he went on to try other swindles and scams but he never achieved the same levels of notoriety again. In 1948, for example, he boasted that he had tried to defraud the Soviet Union of $2 billion ($152 billion in today's money) in a plan to supply the communist empire with gold.

"What a joke on the communists that would have been," he said.

Perhaps it was more of an old man's fantasy than a joke. Ponzi spent the last few years of his life living in Brazil eking out a meagre existence teaching English. He died a pauper in 1949 with savings of $75, just enough to pay his funeral expenses and nothing more.

You may think that Ponzi's life was worthless, but you should think again. His life story is a morality tale. It brilliantly illustrates that the old saying "if it seems too good to be true it probably is" is a rule worth following strictly throughout your life.

Questions

A. "**Whenever** Charles Ponzi **spoke**, people **paid** attention." Are these verbs **(1)** expressing things that happened at a definite time in the past and were finished or **(2)** states that existed in the past or **(6)** things that happened often or regularly, such as habits or **(8)** speculation about the past?

B. "He promised his investors that they **would** double their money in 90 days or, if they were more cautious, he **would** pay them 50 per cent interest for 45 days." This sentence uses the verb **would** twice. Does it express **(6)** a past habit or something that happened regularly or often in the past or **(7)** things that were still in the future or **(8)** speculation about the past or **(9)** things that did not happen, that were hypothetical, unreal or imaginary?

C. Look at the verbs **were gathering** and **would** in the second paragraph. Which one **(3)** expresses something that was still in progress, in other words, unfinished, and which one is **(7)** something that was still in the future?

D. "But what **must have been** even more important, was the fact that he **was prepared** to share his secret with the public." Which of these verbs expresses **(2)** a state that existed in the past and which one expresses or **(8)** speculation about the past?

E. The story says Ponzi told his investors that he **had discovered** a way of making a fortune. Does the verb **had discovered** refer to **(1)** something that happened at a definite time in the past and was finished or is it **(10)** indirect speech for what he said: "I **have discovered** a way of making a fortune"?

F. In the early twentieth century, these coupons **were** used for reply-paid mail. That is, when someone, usually a company, sent correspondence internationally they **would** include the cost of the postage for the reply in the form of a coupon. The two highlighted verbs express the same idea. Is it **(1)** something that happened at a definite time in the past and was finished or **(6)** a past habit or something that happened regularly or often in the past?

G. "Everything **was going** very well for Ponzi, until the authorities and the *Boston Post* newspaper **began** investigating." Which of these highlighted verbs expresses **(1)** something that happened at a definite time in the past and was finished and which one expresses **(3)** something that was still in progress, in other words, unfinished?

H. "Unfortunately for the investors, Ponzi was operating a type of fraud or scam which, in those days, **was known** as 'robbing Peter to pay Paul'." Was this **(1)** something that happened at a definite time in the past and was finished or **(2)** a state that existed in the past?

I. "First it **was not** possible to convert the coupons to cash, as Ponzi claimed, they **could be used** only to buy stamps." Do these highlighted verbs indicate **(1)** things that happened at a definite time in the past and were finished at that time or **(2)** states that existed in the past?

J. "So, even if Ponzi **had been able** to control the whole market in coupons and stamps, he **could not have earned** money in sufficient quantities to sustain his business." Is this **(8)** speculation about the past or **(9)** something that did not happen, in other words hypothetical, unreal or imaginary with hypothetical past consequences?

A … B … C (3) …… (7) …… D (2) …… (8) …… E … F … G (1) …… (3) …… H … I … J …

Summary

In 1920 Charles Ponzi **A …** investment opportunities to the people of Boston in the United States, that seemed too good to be true. Put your money in his Securities Exchange Company, he **B** ... tell people, and he **C** ... double it in 90 days. Ponzi claimed he had discovered a way of making untold millions by manipulating a system of international postal orders which used to operate in those days. Word of his success spread and in less that six months he had raised $15 million, equivalent to billions of dollars in today's money. But then the authorities began investigating. They discovered that there was no way of making money from postal coupons. Rather Ponzi **D** ... a scam known in those days as "robbing Peter to pay Paul" which worked by using money from new investors to pay the old investors. When the investigation began, the new money quickly dried up and the scheme suddenly collapsed. It turned out that it was too good to be true. Ever since then, scams like this **E** ... known as "Ponzi schemes".

(3) was offering (4) have been (5) had been running (6) would (7) would

Scared out of their wits (B2)

The palace of Woodstock in the English county of Oxfordshire doesn't exist anymore but it **used to** be one of the favourite hunting lodges of the kings of England. During the English Civil War in the seventeenth century between the monarchists and the parliamentarians, it became a place of great symbolic importance.

In 1649, after the execution of the king, the parliamentarians **decided** to take control of the palace on behalf of the people. So, they **sent** a commission to put a value on it and the extensive park that surrounded it. The commission **consisted of** four captains from the parliamentary army (Cockaine, Hart, Crook, Carelesse and Roe), a lawyer, a surveyor, a secretary, Giles Sharp and various servants. The group **arrived** at Woodstock on 13 October and **occupied** the two main rooms of the royal apartment which **was** on the first floor.

Throughout their stay they **used** these rooms for sleeping and they **worked** below in the dining room and other rooms. At first everything went well. The officials **were making** progress with their tasks and they felt very comfortable in the house of the late king. Everything was calm and quiet. But their problems were just about to begin.

On the third day of their stay, everything **changed**. When they were dining below on the ground floor in the evening, they **heard** someone moving about in their apartment on the first floor. Whoever it was, **was pacing** back and forth across the room. The sound of the footsteps was very loud and it frightened the men because the rooms on the first floor were locked and chained. No one could enter without a key.

So the four soldiers, the lawyer and the secretary went upstairs to investigate and find out who had succeeded in entering the locked apartment. But there was no one inside. So instead of calming their nerves, this only made them more frightened.

They were so worried that they slept with their candles alight that night. But at midnight, the candles suddenly went out and, in the darkness, they could hear someone in the kitchen downstairs smashing the plates and dishes and throwing the cooking utensils around. What's more, they could smell sulphur.

All the men cowered under their blankets while these strange things were happening and stayed there all night.

This was just the beginning of the terror. When they got up in the morning there was no sign of what had happened during the night. All of the smashed crockery **had disappeared** and all the pots and pans and cooking utensils were back in their proper places.

From then, every night other strange things happened and they **always started** at midnight when the candles suddenly went out. One night lots of stones **were thrown** into the room where the men **were sleeping** and they could hear the glass breaking in the windows. But in the morning, there was no sign of any stones in the room and none of the windows were broken.

On other nights dirty water rained down from the ceiling and one time a monster entered the room and walked around the beds. They could not see very well in the darkness but they thought the monster looked like a great bear or something similar. The monster shook the beds and tugged at the blankets.

Then the explosions started. Many explosions which, at the beginning, sounded like pistol shots but later grew louder and sounded more like cannons. Once there were 19 of these loud cannon shots in a row. They were so loud that everyone living near the palace heard them.

All the men got down on their knees and prayed to God. But the lawyer could not stand it anymore and he fled. He said that he would not stay a moment longer in that haunted palace even if they paid him £500, which is to say millions of dollars in today's money.

He was scared out of his wits, an expression which means very, very frightened. The noun "wits" is used for quick, lively intelligence. So, if you are scared out of your wits, you are so frightened that you cannot think straight.

But the secretary, Giles Sharp, was certainly not scared out of his wits. He was made of sterner stuff. He armed himself with a sword and remained on guard that night with a lighted candle. Everything was quiet and calm until midnight when another monster appeared in the room and snuffed out the candle with his cloven hoof. Sharp **would** say later that it was the Devil himself and the Devil **had attacked** him and taken his sword.

Sharp proved himself to be the bravest of them all because, despite his confrontation with the Devil, he was back on guard the following night when the cannons began firing again. The sparks from the cannons started a fire in the palace and it was Sharp who extinguished the flames. **If it hadn't been** for Sharp, the palace **would have burned** to the ground.

After about three weeks of this terror, the other parliamentarians had had enough. They, too, were scared out of their wits and, like the lawyer had done before, they fled. By then everyone in the neighbouring villages knew about the Devil in the palace and before long news of these strange events spread the length and breadth of the land.

No one was able to contradict the news from Woodstock at the time because nobody had either the facts or the understanding to ask the right questions and express doubts. For many years most people assumed it was all true and that the house was, indeed, haunted by the Devil himself. It was only with the restoration of the monarchy in 1660 that the truth could come to light.

The key to the mystery was Giles Sharp or, better to give him his real name, Joseph Collins, or his nickname, "Funny Joe". Collins was well-known in those parts as a practical joker, hence his nickname. But he **was** also a devoted royalist or monarchist and **had worked** in the Palace of Woodstock as a young man. So he knew the house and all of its secrets very well.

When the parliamentarians arrived to take possession of the royal family's estate, Funny Joe hatched a plan to make them flee using his knowledge of the house and his skills as a practical joker including his knowledge of gunpowder and fireworks.

He got the job as secretary of the commission and included some of his friends in the team of servants. Now everything was ready for the entrance of the Devil to the Palace of Woodstock. Or, better still, the joke of the century.

Funny Joe knew there was a secret trap door in the royal apartment's ceiling which he and his friends could use to come and go as they pleased. They used the trap door to throw stones and broken glass into the room and to spray dirty water over those who were trying to sleep inside. They also used it to tidy up the room before dawn and leave members of the commission in a state of terror and confusion.

The beast that entered the room in the early hours of the morning was not a bear or a devil but a mastiff a type of enormous dog. And, of course, the devil who extinguished the candle when Giles Sharp, or Funny Joe, was standing guard did not exist. The only person who claimed to have seen him was the joker.

But Funny Joe's best tricks were those he played with gunpowder. He used a type called "white powder" which was not very well known in those days. With this powder, he would treat the candles so they would go out of their own accord in a short time and this is why, every night, they all went out at about midnight. He also used it to create delayed explosions and in this way was able to evade suspicion because as far as the officers could see, Giles Sharp shared their experiences and their fears.

In the end, Funny Joe succeeded in driving the parliamentarians away. But the world had to wait decades to learn the truth about how he did it.

But despite his efforts, the palace did not survive the Civil War. It was so badly damaged that eventually it was pulled down. The land was given to the Churchill family who, as the Dukes of Marlborough, would build Blenheim Palace in its place. And one of Blenheim Palace's great claims to fame is that it was the birthplace of Sir Winston Churchill.

Questions

A. The first sentence says the palace at Woodstock **used to** be one of the favourite hunting lodges of the kings of England. Was this (2) a state that existed in the past and is now finished

61

or (6) a past habit or something that happened regularly or often in the past?

B. These are the verbs in paragraph two: **decided**, **sent**, **consisted of**, **arrived**, **occupied** and **was**. Which of these express **(1)** things that happened at a definite time in the past and are finished and which express **(2)** states that existed in the past?

C. Look at the verbs in this sentence: "**Throughout** their stay they **used** these room for sleeping and they **worked** below in the dining room and other rooms". Do they mean **(1)** things that happened at a definite time in the past and were finished at that time or **(6)** a past habit or things that happened regularly or often in the past?

D. The story says the officials **were making** progress. Is this **(1)** something that happened at a definite time in the past and was finished or **(3)** something that was still in progress, in other words, unfinished?

E. The story tells us that on the third day everything **changed**, the men **heard** noises upstairs and someone **was pacing** back and forth. Which of these verbs expresses something **(1)** that happened at a definite time in the past and was finished and which expresses **(3)** something that was still in progress, in other words, unfinished?

F. When the story says the smashed crockery **had disappeared** is it referring to **(1)** something that happened at a definite time in the past and was finished or **(5)** something that happened before something else in the past?

G. The three highlighted verbs in this extract each have a different meaning: "From then, every night more strange things happened and they **always started** at midnight when the candles suddenly went out. One night lots of stones **were thrown** into the room where the men **were sleeping** and they could hear the glass breaking in the windows". Which of the verbs means **(1)** something that happened at a definite time in the past and was finished and which means **(3)** something that was still in progress, in other words, unfinished, and, finally, which one means **(6)** a past habit or something that happened regularly or often in the past?

H. Look at the verbs in this sentence: "Sharp **would** say later that it was the Devil himself and the Devil **had attacked** him and taken his sword". Which one expresses **(5)** something that happened before something else in the past and which one expresses **(7)** something that was still in the future?

I. "**If it hadn't been** for Sharp, the palace **would have burned** to the ground." Does this sentence convey the meaning of **(8)** speculation about the past or **(9)** something that did not happen, in other words something hypothetical, unreal or imaginary with hypothetical past consequences?

J. Look at the verbs in this sentence: "But he **was** also a devoted royalist or monarchist and **had worked** in the Palace of Woodstock as a young man". Which one expresses **(2)** a state that existed at a definite time in the past and was finished and **(5)** something that happened before something else in the past.

A ... B (1) ...... (2) ...... C ...... D ...... E (1) ...... (3)......
F ... G (1) ...... (3) ...... (6) ...... H (5) ...... (7) ...... I ... J
(1) ...... (5) ......

Summary

In the English Civil War, which was fought between the royalists and the parliamentarians, the royal palace at Woodstock in the county of Oxfordshire became a place of great symbolic importance. After the execution of the king in 1649, a party of parliamentarians **A ...** there to take. They **B ...** they would have an easy time of it but they were very much mistaken. Not long after they arrived strange things started happening at night. Water poured over them from the ceiling, pots and pans were rattled and glass windows smashed. But when they got up in the morning everything **C ...** cleared away. The trouble always **D ...** around midnight when their candles suddenly went out for no reason. On one occasion a monster entered their sleeping quarters and prowled around and at other times there were loud explosions during the night which were also heard in the nearby village. It wasn't too long before the parliamentary officials fled in terror. The palace was obviously haunted by the Devil himself. It **E ...** be until long after the war ended that the truth came out. The haunting was not the work of the Devil but of a well-known local practical joker and royalist Joseph Collins, or "Funny Joe" to his friends. Funny Joe had worked at the palace in his youth and he knew all of its secret passages and trap doors which he used, with his knowledge of gunpowder, to create the terrifying effects that drove the parliamentarians away.

(1) went (5) had been (6) started (7) would not (8) must have thought

Raise your glasses (B2+)

Champagne is famous for its bubbles and its sparkle. It lifts the spirits and is the drink of choice for every kind of celebration: weddings, sporting victories and New Year's Eve all dance to the music of popping corks and champagne fizz. As often as not, when someone says "raise your glasses" to toast a newly married couple, some great success or just bright hopes for the future, those glasses will be full of Champagne.

It seems like Champagne **has been** with us always. And indeed, it has. They **have been making** wine in the Champagne region of France since the days of the Roman Empire. But it **has not always been** a fizzy white wine like it is now.

On the contrary, they originally **used to make** still, red wine in Champagne. How and why they changed to making the white, bubbly wine that is so famous today is a matter of historical controversy.

Vincent Cronin, in his biography of Louis XIV, mentions one of the most popular stories about the origins of Champagne which is that it **was invented** by a Benedictine monk, Dom Perignon, in 1670. Certainly, Dom Perignon had something to do with it and one of the most luxurious and famous brands of Champagne still bears his name. But the story is much more complicated.

Long before the days of Louis XIV and Dom Perignon, Champagne wine makers knew their red wine was never going to be as good as the red wines of Burgundy further south because of the cooler climate in their region, so they switched to making white wine instead.

But still, there were problems. Champagne's cool climate meant the grapes did not fully ripen and fermentation was delayed. So, once the wine was bottled and put in the cellars, it **would** undergo a secondary fermentation which produced carbon dioxide bubbles. These bubbles caused pressure to build up inside the bottles, and sometimes they **would** explode. One estimate says as many as 90 per cent of the bottles blew up in this way.

Not only was this physically dangerous, but economically disastrous as well. Not only were the wine makers losing a lot of their product but French people at the time did not like wine with bubbles in it. This was considered a failing rather than a virtue.

Clearly, something needed to be done. And this is where Dom Perignon came into the story, but he **wasn't trying** to create a sparkling wine, as the original story says, rather he **was trying** to prevent the secondary fermentation. But fortunately, he failed and so, the wine makers of Champagne continued to produce their distinctive, fizzy wine which might not have been to the taste of French wine lovers, but on the other side of the English Channel, they loved it.

Many of the people who **have written** about Champagne's fascinating history argue it was the English taste for the fizzy drink in the late eighteenth century that transformed it from an unremarkable wine into the fabulous, luxurious and happy drink that we know today.

But, of course, there are many other factors and people who influenced the story along the way and one of the most famous of them was Barbe-Nicole Ponsardin, who married Francois

Clicquot, heir to a famous wine-making family. When Francois died in 1806, Barbe-Nicole at the age of just 27 took over the family firm. Despite her youth and inexperience, not to mention that fact that she **was working** in what was very much a man's world, she **made** Clicquot one of the most famous brands of Champagne. A bottle is instantly recognisable today with its distinctive orange label and the brand "Veuve Clicquot-Ponsardin" or "The Widow Clicquot-Ponsardin".

Such is the fame of the brand that some people in the English-speaking world refer to champagne simply as "the widow". Others call it "bubbly" or "fizz" or "champers" for obvious reasons.

But there is another nickname that is not so obvious: "the boy". The story goes that at an aristocratic shooting party in Britain in the nineteenth century, there was a boy who carried an ice bucket with bottles of champagne in case any of the shooters felt like a drink. One of the guests at the party was the Prince of Wales, a pleasure-loving man of gargantuan appetites. The prince, who **would become** King Edward VII when his mother Queen Victoria died, **would shout** "where's the boy" whenever he wanted a drink, which was quite often. And so "the boy" **became** synonymous with champagne, at least in some circles.

So, the next time you raise your glass to toast a success, or a happy couple who have just got married, or the next New Year's Eve, spare a thought for the monk, the widow, the anonymous boy and all those thousands of people down through the ages who helped to make fabulous champagne what it is today. **If they had not done** what they did, these celebrations **might not be** quite so much fun nowadays.

Questions

A. Look at the verbs **has been**, **have been making**, and **has not always been** in the second paragraph. Do they verbs refer to **(1)** things that happened at a definite time in the past and were finished, or **(4)** things from an unspecified or indefinite time the past but which, in some way, still affect the present?

B. When the story says "they **used to make** still, red wine" does it mean **(1)** something that happened at a definite time in the past and was finished or **(6)** a past habit or something that happened regularly or often in the past?

C. The story says Champagne **was invented** by Dom Perignon, in 1670. Was this **(1)** something that happened at a definite time in the past and was finished or **(3)** something that was still in progress, in other words, unfinished?

D. The story says Champagne **would** undergo a secondary fermentation and sometimes the bottles **would** explode. Does **would** in this context express **(6)** a past habit or something that happened regularly or often in the past, **(7)** something that was still in the future, **(8)** speculation about the past or, finally, does it express **(9)** something that did not happen, in other words something hypothetical, unreal or imaginary?

E. Dom Perignon **wasn't trying** to create a sparkling wine but **was trying** to prevent the secondary fermentation. Do these verbs refer to **(1)** something that happened at a definite time in the past and was finished or **(3)** something that was still in progress, in other words, unfinished?

F. When the story says many people **have written** about the history of Champagne is it referring to **(1)** something that happened at a definite time in the past and was finished or something **(4)** from an unspecified or indefinite time in the past which, in some way, still affects the present?

G. This sentence is an example of a common pattern in which an action in progress is interrupted by an action that was completed: "Despite her youth and inexperience, not to mention that fact that she **was working** in what was very much a man's world, she **made** Clicquot one of the most famous brands of Champagne". Which verb expresses **(1)** something that happened at a definite time in the past and was finished and which one expresses **(3)** something that was still in progress, in other words, unfinished?

H. The verb **would** appears in this sentence twice, each time expressing a different meaning: "The prince, who **would become** King Edward VII when his mother Queen Victoria died, **would shout** "where's the boy" whenever he wanted a drink, which was quite often". Which one expresses (6) a past habit or something that happened regularly or often in the past and which one (7) something that was still in the future?

I. When the story says "the boy" **became** synonymous with champagne is it referring to **(1)** something that happened at a definite time in the past and was finished or **(3)** something that was still in progress, in other words, unfinished?

J. Look at the last sentence: "**If they had not done** what they did, these celebrations **might not be** quite so much fun nowadays". Is this a reference to **(1)** something that happened at a definite time in the past and was finished or **(9)** something unreal, hypothetical or imaginary in the past with hypothetical consequences in the present?

A … B … C … D … E … F … G (1) …… (3) …… H(6)…… (7) …… I … J …

Summary

The story of champagne is tied up with a monk, a widow and a boy. The monk's name **A …** Dom Perignon who is widely credited with inventing champagne which is not quite true. His contribution to the story of Champagne was that he tried and failed to control the fermentation process. Nevertheless, his memory is preserved on the labels of one of the most famous Champagne brands. The widow's name was Barbe Nicole Ponsardin. She **B ...** Francois Cliquot, the heir to a famous family of wine makers in Champagne. When he died in 1806, she was just 27 years old, but she took over the business and succeeded in turning Cliquot into another famous Champagne brand. As with the monk, her name is preserved on the labels to this day: Veuve Cliquot Ponsardin, the word "veuve" meaning "widow" in English. And finally, there was the boy. Unfortunately, we don't know his name, he was just a lad who carried an ice bucket full of Champagne at an aristocratic shooting party in England. The aristocrats apparently liked to drink, even while they **C ...** . The Prince of Wales, who **D ...** later become Edward VII, was at the party and whenever he wanted more champagne he **E ...** shout "where's the boy". After that in some aristocratic circles, Champagne became known as "the boy". Others call it "the widow" but most people use words such as "bubbles", "bubbly" or "fizz".

(1) Married (2) was (3) were shooting (6) would (7) would

The last straw (B2+)

The shortest academic exam in all history must surely be the oral chemistry exam of James Whistler at the US West Point Military Academy in 1854. By all accounts, it lasted less than 30 seconds. Whistler was asked to discuss the nature of silicon, which is a rock crystal. "Silicon is a gas," **was** Whistler's answer and with that, the exam was over.

Not only did he fail chemistry, but he **suffered** the humiliation of being expelled from West Point. This might seem an unduly harsh punishment for failing just one exam but in fact Whistler **was constantly** in trouble during his time at the academy. You could say the failure was "the last straw" meaning that he had caused so many problems that the army **would** tolerate him no longer. This is a commonly shortened form of an old expression "the straw that broke the camel's back," meaning that after a succession of bad things, something quite minor can be intolerable.

Years later, Whistler would say, "**had silicon been** a gas, I **would have been** a major general". Luckily, he had another string to his bow – an expression which means another talent or skill that he could use. His other talent was art. He had always been interested in art and after his expulsion he had time to pursue a career in painting.

And what a career it turned out to be! He **became** one of the most famous artists of the late nineteenth century. His most famous painting, which hangs in the Musee d'Orsay in Paris, is called "Arrangement in Grey and Black No. 1" but is commonly known as "Portrait of Whistler's Mother".

NOTE: "Whistler's Mother" has a supporting role in the 1997 comedy film *Bean: The Ultimate Disaster Movie* when the clumsy Mr Bean manages to destroy it in a hilarious slapstick scene.

Questions

A. Was Whistler's answer to the exam questions something **(1)** that happened at a definite time in the past and was finished or **(3)** something that was still in progress, in other words, unfinished?

B. When he **suffered** the humiliation of being expelled, was his suffering (2) a state that existed in the past or (3) something that was still in progress, in other words, unfinished?

C. The story says Whistler "**was constantly** in trouble during his time at the academy". Was this **(1)** something that happened at a definite time in the past and were finished or **(6)** a past habit or something that happened regularly or often in the past?

D. The story says that after Whistler failed his exam, the army "**would** tolerate him no longer". Does **would** in this context mean **(6)** a past habit or something that happened regularly or often or **(7)** something that was still in the future or **(8)** speculation about the past or **(9)** something unreal or imaginary in the past with a hypothetical consequence in the past?

E. Was Whistler's statement "**had silicon been** a gas, I **would have been** a major general" **(6)** a past habit or something that happened regularly or often or **(7)** something that was still in the future or **(8)** speculation about the past or **(9)** something unreal or imaginary in the past with a hypothetical consequence in the past?

F. Was Whistler's transformation into a great artist something **(1)** that happened at a definite time in the past or something **(9)** unreal or imaginary in the past?

A … B … C … D … E … F …

Summary

James Whistler, a military cadet at the West Point Academy in the United States, **A …** always in trouble. Then, in 1854, he failed his oral chemistry exam in record time. The first question was to discuss the nature of silicon, to which he replied that silicon **B …** a gas. He was wrong, silicon is in fact a rock crystal and with that, the exam was over and his military career too. It seems that his failure in the exam was the last straw and Whistler **C …** . It turned out that this was the making of him. He **D …** a talented artist and **E …** to become one of the most famous painters of the late nineteenth century.

(1) was expelled (2) was (5) had always been (7) would go on (10) was

When royal heads rolled (B2+)

In early 1745 a Scottish gentleman by the name of Charles Edward Stuart **established** a Masonic lodge in the town of Arras in northern France. Stuart **had spent** six months in the town and the lodge was his way of saying thank you for all the hospitality.

Among the officers **appointed** by Stuart was a local lawyer and businessman called Maximilien Robespierre. At the time there **was** nothing in common between the Scottish gentleman and the French lawyer other than their interest in the Masons. But within half a century a strange connection **would be forged** which, in retrospect, made their encounter in Arras a bizarre footnote in human history.

Stuart was the great grandson of a king who **was** executed. Robespierre was the grandfather of a man who **would** execute a king. Stuart's great grandfather **was** Charles I of England whose death was ordered by Parliament in 1649 during the English Civil War for trying to make himself a tyrant. Robespierre's grandson **was** the famous French revolutionary leader Maximilien Robespierre another lawyer from Arras who, more than anyone, was responsible for the death of King Louis XVI on charges of treachery on 21 January 1793.

The methods used to carry out the sentences were different: the former **was killed** by a man wielding an axe and the latter by the guillotine. But in both cases the result was the same, their heads rolled, an expression meaning that their heads were cut off. Nowadays the same expression is used metaphorically to describe what happens when people are sacked from their jobs because of serious mistakes or failures.

Questions

A. Look at the verbs **established** and **had spent** in the first paragraph. Which one expresses **(1)** something that happened at a definite time in the past and was finished and which one expresses **(5)** something in the past that happened before something else in the past?

B. Look at the verbs **appointed**, **was** and **would be forged** in the second paragraph. Which one expresses **(1)** something that happened in the past and was finished, which one expresses **(2)** a state that existed in the past and which one expresses something **(7)** that was still in the future?

C. Robespierre was the grandfather of a man who **would** execute a king. Stuart was the great grandson of a king who **was** executed. Which of these events was **(1)** something that happened at a definite time in the past and was finished and which **(7)** was still in the future?

D. The story says Stuart's grandfather **was** King Charles I and Robespierre's grandson **was** the revolutionary also called Maximilien Robespierre. Does **was** in this context signify something **(1)** that happened at a definite time in the past and was finished or **(2)** a state that existed in the past?

E. The story says Charles **was killed** with an axe and Louis by the guillotine. Does **was killed** signify **(1)** something that happened at a definite time in the past and was finished or **(2)** a state that existed for a time in the past?

A (1) ... (5) ... B (1) ... (2) ... (7) ... C (1) ... (7) ... D ... E ...

Summary

In 1745 there **A** ... nothing remarkable about a meeting in the French city of Arras between Charles Edward Stuart and a lawyer called Maximilien Robespierre. But in hindsight the meeting forms a bizarre footnote to history. Stuart, better known by his nickname "Bonnie Prince Charlie", **B** ... the great grandson of a king who **C** .... Robespierre was the grandfather of a man who **D** ... execute a king. Stuart's great grandfather, Charles I was executed in 1649 during the English Civil War. Robespierre's grandson, also called Maximilien, **E** ... King Louis XVI of France during the French Revolution.

(1) executed (1) was executed (2) was (2) was (7) would

The fruits of his labour (B2+)

The expression "the fruits of one's labour" means the result and reward that you get for your hard work. It is a metaphor, it does not mean you get fruit, it could be money or fame or just the satisfaction of having achieved something or created something.

But, in the case of Hayward Wright, a horticulturalist in early twentieth century New Zealand, the fruits of his labour really were fruit: Kiwifruit. This delicious fruit, with its brown furry skin and sweet green flesh, is one of New Zealand's most famous exports even though it did not originally come from New Zealand, it **came** from China. The original, which was known as the Chinese gooseberry, was a wild plant and the fruit was much smaller than a Kiwifruit and with smooth, green skin rather than brown, furry skin. A New Zealand school teacher called Mary Fraser, who **went** to visit her sister in China, brought cuttings of Chinese gooseberry with her when she **returned** home in 1904.

It became a popular plant in New Zealand and remained unchanged until the 1920s when Wright, through a process of selective breeding, transformed it into the fruit that is world-famous today. In the last part of the twentieth century and into the twenty-first century, the Kiwifruit industry **has grown** into a multi-billion-dollar industry. It is now New Zealand's biggest horticultural export – horticulture is the type of agriculture that produces fruit and vegetables. Not only that, but since the 1990s many other countries around the world, including China, **have been growing** their own.

If Hayward Wright had lived into the twenty-first century, he **would have been** proud to see the fruits of his labour incorporated into the cuisines of many different countries and many different dishes, especially desserts.

Questions

A. The story says kiwifruit originally **came** from China. Is this **(1)** something that happened at a definite time in the past and was finished or **(2)** a state that existed in the past?

B. Mary Fraser **went** to China and **returned** to New Zealand in 1904. Were these **(1)** things that she did at definite times in the past and were finished or **(2)** states that existed in the past?

C. When the story says "the Kiwifruit industry **has grown**" does this mean **(1)** something that happened at a definite time in the past and was finished or **(3)** something that was still in progress, in other words, unfinished, or **(4)** something from an unspecified or indefinite time in the past that still affects the present in some way?

D. Look at this quote from the story "since the 1990s many other countries around the world, including China, **have been growing** their own". Does this verb refer to **(1)** something that happened at a definite time in the past and was finished or something **(4)** from a period of time beginning in the 1990s which affects the present?

E. Look at this quote from the story: "**If Hayward Wright had lived** into the twenty-first century, he **would have been** proud". Does it express **(8)** speculation about the past or something **(9)** that did not happen, in other words something hypothetical, unreal or imaginary with hypothetical past consequences?

A ... B ... C ... D ... E ...

Summary

In 1904 Mary Fraser, a schoolteacher, returned to New Zealand from a visit to China bringing with her samples of a plant **A ...** the Chinese gooseberry. Over the next twenty years these plants, with their green, smooth-skinned berries became popular among New Zealand gardeners. But then, Hayward Wright, who **B ...** as a horticulturist, **C ...** a process of selective breeding that transformed the Chinese gooseberry into the Kiwifruit which had brown, furry skin and was much larger than the original. Since then, it **D ......** one of New Zealand's most important exports and many other countries, including China, **E......** their own since the 1990s.

(1) began (2) known as (3) was working (4) has become (4) have been growing

Nothing new under the sun (B2+)

The Olympic Games has its own, special set of ideals. They are expressed in the Olympic creed which says, "The most important thing in the Olympic Games is not to win but to take part, just as the most important thing in life is not the triumph but the struggle. The essential thing is not to **have conquered** but to **have fought** well."

Every four years the athletes of the world assemble to compete and many of them live up to the ideal. Many, but not all. Hardly an Olympic Games goes by without some showing their ideals are the opposite. To them, the important thing is not to take part but to win at all costs even if they must cheat. Their methods are well-known, performance enhancing drugs are by far the most common but the use of violence against opponents and bribery are not unknown.

It is tempting to conclude that money is to blame. Some athletes lose their sense of morality because an Olympic victory is not just about the glory and the honour, it can make the victor wealthy. Many people **have argued** that this is the fault of the modern world and we should go back to the Olympic Games as they **were** in ancient Greece when things **were** simpler, uncorrupted by money and much closer the ideal.

Unfortunately, there is nothing new under the sun as they **would have found out if they had read** a little more ancient history. Ancient sources have many references to cheating at the games. For example, in the 98th Olympiad, which **took place** about 2500 years ago, a boxer called Eupolos **was fined** for bribing his opponents to let him win. Today, in boxing circles, this is known as "taking a dive".

Bronze statues of Eupolos and the men he **bribed were erected** at Olympia, not to honour them but to shame them and to warn other athletes not to try any dirty tricks of their own. The statues have long since disappeared but we know about them because hundreds of years later, a Greek travel writer by the name of Pausanias **visited** Olympia and **retold** the story about this early Olympic cheating scandal using the inscriptions on the statues as his source of information.

In his book, he **noted** that one inscription read: "Not with money, but swiftness of foot and bodily vigour, ought one to win prizes at Olympia".

NOTE: The expression "nothing new under the sun" comes from the book of Ecclesiastes in the *Bible*.

What has been is what will be,

And what has been done is what will be done;

And there is nothing new under the sun.

Questions

A. The Olympic oath, quoted in the first paragraph, states "the essential thing is not to **have conquered** but to **have fought** well". Do these verbs refer to **(1)** things that happened at a definite time in the past and were finished or **(4)** things from unspecified or indefinite times in the past that, in some way, still affect the present?

B. When the story says many people **have argued** that cheating is a modern phenomenon, is **have argued** referring to **(1)** something that happened at a definite time in the past and was finished or **(4)** something that happened at an unspecified or indefinite time in the past but which, in some way, affects the present?

C. Paragraph three talks about the games as they **were** in ancient Greece, a time when things **were** simpler and uncorrupted by money. Do these verbs refer to **(1)** things that happened at a definite time in the past and were finished at that time, **(2)** states that existed in the past or **(6)** past habits or things that happened regularly or often in the past?

D. When the story says "they **would have found out if they had read** a little more ancient history", is it expressing **(6)** a past habit or something that happened regularly or often in the past, **(7)** something that was still in the future, **(8)** speculation about the past or **(9)** something that did not happen, in other words, something hypothetical, unreal or imaginary with hypothetical past consequences?

E. These verbs from the last three paragraphs **took place**, **was fined**, **bribed**, **were erected**, **visited**, **retold** and **noted** have something in common. Is it that they all express **(1)** things that happened at definite times in the past and were finished at those times, **(2)** states that existed in the past, **(3)** things that were still in progress, in other words, unfinished, or **(4)** things that happened at unspecified or indefinite times in the past and still, in some way, affect the present?

A ... B ... C ... D ... E ...

Summary

Many people think that cheating at the Olympic Games is something new but it is not. Athletes **A ...** to gain an unfair advantage at the Games ever since they began in ancient Greece. Nowadays the usual form of cheating is through performance enhancing drugs but in the old days it **B ...** bribery. For instance, in the 98th Olympiad, 2500 years ago, a boxer called Eupolos

C...... for paying money to his opponents to let him win by "taking a dive". When they were caught, the authorities at Olympia erected statues in bronze of the cheats to publicly shame them. Although the statues disappeared a long time ago, an ancient Greek travel writer called Pausanias described them in his book. **D ...** for Pausanias, we **D ...** anything about this. But fortunately, Pausanias not only described the statues but he **E ......** the inscriptions on them. "Not with money, but with swiftness of foot and bodily vigour, ought one to win prizes at Olympia," said one.

(1) was fined (1) recorded (2) was (4) have been trying (9)If it had not been ... would not know

The diamond sting (B2+)

On a farm in the Champagne region of France in the eighteenth century lived a barefoot country girl called Jeanne de Saint-Remy who **worked night and day** and often went hungry. Jeanne believed that she was really a princess and her rightful place was at the top of the social ladder rather than mucking out the cows on her father's farm.

Surprising as it may seem, she **was** right. She **was**, indeed, a direct descendant of Henry II, the last king of the Valois dynasty and, after her father's death, through a series of lucky breaks plus sheer willpower she **managed** to put her case to King Louis XVI who **granted** her a royal pension.

It was enough to enable her to have small apartments in Paris and at Versailles but Jeanne wanted more. She did not want to be an insignificant moth fluttering on the outskirts of the most glittering court in Europe. No, she wanted to be right at the centre of it as a fully-fledged princess.

But to do that Jeanne – who the great historian Thomas Carlyle described as having a "face of some piquancy" – needed money and lots of it, so she came up with a plan. What she did was organise an elaborate type of confidence trick known in United States' slang as a "sting". It seems that, as well as her royal bloodlines, she **had inherited** from somewhere the quick wit and instincts of a con artist.

First, she needed real psychological insight to pick the right person to be the victim, known in the trade as "the mark". Not just anyone would do. Obviously, it had to be someone with money but there needed to be an inner weakness or desire that she could exploit to turn the mark against himself.

Then she needed a high degree of organisational skill to create an illusion into which the mark **would be lured** so that he could be manipulated and relieved of large amounts of cash – the sting. Much like a stage magician she **would have to** do it by playing tricks and creating distractions.

But the skills she required were of a much higher order than those of a mere conjurer. In the theatre, the magician controls every detail and the audience know they are being tricked, it's all part of the fun. But the con artist cannot control everything and it is essential that the audience in this type of illusion remain unaware of what is really happening.

Jeanne found her mark in 1784. His name was Cardinal Rohan, one of the richest men in France. She befriended him and soon discovered his hidden weakness, the desire for power. Although he was already a powerful man, he wanted more but his ambitions **were being** blocked by the Queen, Marie Antoinette. She disdained him because many years before he had insulted her mother and she had never forgiven him.

With the Queen keeping the Cardinal at arm's length he was finding it almost impossible to take his place at the centre of the court of Versailles and he was prepared to do almost anything, pay almost any price, to make amends and ingratiate himself with her.

Armed with this useful knowledge, Jeanne, by now married and sometimes referred to as Countess La Motte, set about creating the illusion that would trick the Cardinal into handing over large sums of money.

Like all scams, it began with a hook, something to get the mark interested. For her hook, Jeanne showed the Cardinal a series of letters she had received from Marie Antoinette which mentioned him in a positive light. Of course, the letters were forgeries. Their only purpose was to get the Cardinal interested and they worked perfectly. From that moment he was hooked.

Next, Jeanne suggested he should write to the Queen, which he did. And before long another forged letter arrived, this time addressed to the Cardinal. It promised him his long-desired audience but it was not possible now so he should be patient and, above all, be discreet. Thus, the Cardinal was not only hooked but forced to keep everything secret.

The Cardinal thought that he was acting in his own interests and those of the Queen by keeping his mouth shut. But, again, he was working against himself. Secrecy was essential to the illusion. **If word had leaked out**, the Cardinal **would soon have discovered** that the Queen had not changed her attitude to him, not one little bit.

But the secret didn't leak. Rohan held it tight enabling Jeanne to start reeling him in. She did this by arranging for him to have a brief meeting with the Queen one moonlit night in a garden at Versailles. The meeting took place 11 August 1785 in a secluded grove outside the palace.

Rohan went to where he was told and found the Queen in a long white dress and a broad brimmed hat with a veil standing alone. He **was trembling** with excitement and **knelt** to kiss the hem of her dress. She passed him a red rose and said words to the effect that he would know what it meant. Before the conversation could go any further Jeanne and an accomplice emerged from the shadows and sounded the alarm that the courtiers **were coming** and everyone better leave. Rohan **hurried** away not realising that the woman in white was not the

Queen but a Parisian prostitute whom Jeanne had paid handsomely for a few minutes work as an impersonator.

The illusion was now complete and Jeanne could land her catch. Shortly afterwards Rohan received two more forged letters from the Queen asking him to contribute generously to her favourite charitable causes. He could pass the money to Jeanne who would see that it reached the people it was intended for.

He was only too happy to oblige and two months after the night meeting, Jeanne had 150,000 French livres, enough money to buy herself a chateau in her native Champagne and embark on leading a lavish lifestyle at court. Rohan, meantime, continued believing that he was back in the Queen's favour and was completely unaware that he had been conned. But Jeanne hadn't finished with him yet.

Just as she was pocketing her profits from the first scam, another sucker turned up. His name was Charles Bohmer and he too had a weakness that it was all too easy for Jeanne to spot: he wanted money. Bohmer was a jeweller who had planned to make his fortune by crafting the most fabulous diamond necklace the world had ever seen for Madame du Barry, who was at the time the lover of the previous king, Louis XV.

He duly made the necklace which was enormous. It had 647 diamonds and weighed 2800 carats, which is more than half a kilo and a price tag to match: 1.6 million livres. Unfortunately for Bohmer, Louis XV died before he could seal the deal and du Barry was banished from the court. Bohmer was left on the verge of financial ruin with huge debts and a very limited market for such a valuable object.

His only chance of financial salvation was the new Queen. Marie Antoinette had a reputation for frivolity, extravagance and loving bright, shiny ornaments. But diamonds just weren't her thing. She was more interested in pearls and declined the offer. At one point the desperate jeweller got down on his knees and begged her buy the necklace and save him from ruin. But in a let-them-eat-cake type of moment she brushed him off and suggested that he break up the necklace and sell the diamonds individually for what they were worth.

Jeanne knew all this and realised she had a new mark to add to the illusion that she had created with Rohan. She passed Rohan another forged letter purportedly from the Queen. It said she desired the necklace but, as she was short of cash and didn't want the King to know about her new extravagance, she wondered if her faithful courtier Rohan might stump up the money. She would pay him back later, of course.

Rohan would do anything to please her majesty so, he paid Bohmer for the necklace and took it to Jeanne's apartment where it was collected by someone he thought was a servant of the Queen. But, of course, the servant was really just another of Jeanne's accomplices.

Jeanne now had everything she needed to live the life of a real princess. The money and the jewels. However, she would never be able to wear the necklace in public because that would give the game away. For the same reason they couldn't sell it. So, she and her husband decided to break it up and sell the diamonds separately in London. They made more than 200,000 livres and still expected to get more as the hapless Rohan paid for the necklace in instalments over the next year or so.

It seemed like another perfect con. All the pieces had neatly fallen into place but there was a problem. An essential part of every con was the illusion, the secrecy. If the spell of the illusion was broken, if someone realised that something didn't add up, then the con would be discovered. And that's exactly what happened.

The first one to suspect something was up, was Rohan who, after some months, could not help noticing that the Queen **had never worn** the diamonds. Bohmer, too, was puzzled when he did not receive an acknowledgement from the Queen that she **had received** the necklace.

He was the one who uncovered the scam when he passed the Queen a note saying how delighted he was that, after all, she **had agreed** to buy it. The Queen was puzzled and smelt a rat. She alerted the King who initiated an investigation which uncovered the scam.

There was a trial in which Rohan was acquitted. As he said himself, he had to employ all his intelligence to persuade his judges that he was a fool. Jeanne was not so lucky. She was convicted and sentenced to be branded with the letter V for "voleuse" or thief and life in prison. However, she managed to escape to England and exacted her revenge on the Queen by publishing her memoirs in which she alleged the Queen and Rohan **had been** lovers.

The memoirs sold well and doubtless she made a lot of money from them, but it would hardly have compensated her for the life that she **had desired** as a wealthy, royal princess at the Palace of Versailles. The problem for Jeanne was that, like her marks, she had a weakness which worked against her and brought about her downfall.

In fact, her weakness was a combination of those that afflicted Rohan and Bohmer: she too wanted to be at the centre of court life, like Rohan and she too wanted money, like Bohmer. And like them, she wanted too much and so overplayed her hand. Flushed with her success in the first con, she couldn't resist trying again when she heard about the diamond necklace. **If she hadn't tried** it a second time, she **might have gotten away** with it.

NOTE: Well worth watching is the highly successful 1973 film *The Sting*, starring Robert Redford and Paul Newman. It is about two con artists in 1930s Chicago who swindle a gangster boss through a sting as elaborate as the one Jeanne worked in eighteenth-century France.

Questions

A. The first sentence says Jeanne de Saint-Remy **worked night and day**. Is this something **(1)** that she did once at a definite time in the past and was finished or **(6)** a past habit or something that she did regularly or often in the past?

B. Now look at the highlighted verbs in the second paragraph: **was**, **was**, **managed** and **granted**. Which of these verbs express **(1)** something that happened at a definite time in the past and was finished and which express **(2)** a state that existed in the past?

C. When the story says she **had inherited** the quick instincts of a con artist does it mean **(1)** something that happened at a definite time in the past which was finished or **(5)** something that happened before something else in the past, that is, the time she made her plan to get more money?

D. The story says the mark **would be lured** and that Jeanne **would have to** play tricks and create distractions. Does **would** in this context express **(6)** a past habit or something that happened regularly or often in the past, **(7)** something that was still in the future, **(8)** speculation about the past or, finally, was it **(9)** something that did not happen, in other words something hypothetical, unreal or imaginary with hypothetical past consequences?

E. Cardinal Rohan's ambitions **were being** blocked by the Queen, Marie Antoinette. Was this **(1)** something that happened a definite time in the past and was finished or **(3)** was it something still in progress, in other words, unfinished?

F. Look at this sentence from the story: "**If word had leaked out**, the Cardinal **would soon have discovered** that the Queen had not changed her attitude to him, not one little bit". Does it refer to **(5)** something that happened before something else in the past or **(7)** something that was still in the future at the time or **(9)** something that did not happen, in other words was hypothetical, unreal or imaginary with hypothetical past consequences?

G. "He **was trembling** with excitement and **knelt** to kiss the hem of her dress." Which of these verbs **(1)** expresses something that happened at a definite time in the past and was finished and which **(3)** expresses an action that was in progress at that time and unfinished?

H. The story says Rohan **hurried** away from his meeting with the fake queen when he heard that the courtiers **were coming**. Which of these verbs **(1)** expresses something that happened at a definite time in the past and was finished and which **(3)** expresses an action that was still in progress, in other words, unfinished?

I. When the story describes how the scam was finally exposed it uses the following verbs: **had never worn**, **had received**, **had agreed**, **had been** and **had desired**. Do these verbs express **(1)** things that happened at definite times in the past and were finished or **(5)** things that happened before other things in the past?

J. "**If she hadn't tried** it a second time, she **might have gotten away** with it." Does this mean **(5)** something that happened before something else in the past or **(7)** something that was still in the future or **(9)** something that did not happen, in

94

other words was hypothetical, unreal or imaginary with hypothetical past consequences?

A ... **B** (1) ...... (2) ...... **C** ... **D** ... **E** ... **F** ... **G** (1) ...... (3) ...... **H** (1) ...... (3) ...... **I** ... **J** ...

Summary

Jeanne de Saint Remy **A** ... a French countess who became one of the greatest con artists in history. She was a natural, she seemed to know instinctively how to target the weaknesses of her victims and to persuade them to hand over large amounts of money. In the 1780s she **B** ... two of the most spectacular confidence tricks in history. Her first victim was Cardinal Rohan whose weakness was the desire for power. Even though the high office of cardinal made him a powerful man, he was not satisfied. He wanted to increase his influence at the court with Queen Marie Antoinette. Unfortunately for him, the queen did not want to have anything to do with him because years before he **C** ...... her mother. Knowing all this, Jeanne used a series of forged letters to persuade him that the queen **D** ...... her mind. When he was convinced, she used the fake letters to ask him for money for the queen's favourite charities. Such was his eagerness to please Marie Antoinette that he gladly paid over large sums of money even though he never got to meet the queen in person. The weakness of Jeanne's second victim was the love of money. Charles Bohmer was a jeweller who wanted to sell the queen an enormous diamond necklace. But the queen was not interested partly because she did not like diamonds and partly because she was aware that she had a bad reputation for extravagance. Again, knowing this, Jeanne exploited both Bohmer and the cardinal when she persuaded the cardinal to buy the necklace on behalf of the queen. It was a double win for Jeanne because she had the money from the cardinal as well as the necklace. Obviously, she **E ...** be able to wear it, so she took it to London and sold the diamonds separately. She might have gotten away with it but, unfortunately for her, Bohmer asked the queen why she had never worn the necklace and with that, the game was up.

(1) pulled off (2) was (5) had insulted (5) had changed (7)would not

Punctured pride (C1)

It was a day of triumph for Queen Elizabeth I of England. One of her favourite sea captains **had just returned** from a voyage around the world with a cargo of treasure. The sailor was Francis Drake, one of the most famous characters in English history and he gave the queen almost all the treasure which, according to measureingworth.com, would be worth about US$565 billion in today's money making her richer that Elon Musk, Bill Gates and Jeff Bezos put together.

However, her advisers warned her not to accept the gift. You see, Drake was a pirate and he had plundered the treasure from Spanish ships in the Americas. If she took it, they said, she **would** risk war with Spain, then the most powerful country in Europe.

For their part, the Spaniards **were watching** events in England very closely to see what the Queen **would** do. Bernadino Mendoza, the Spanish ambassador to the court of Elizabeth, wrote to King Phillip II of Spain to describe what happened.

Instead of doing what her advisers had suggested, she went to the port of Deptford near London on 4 April 1581, to celebrate Drake's success with a banquet on board his ship *The Golden Hind* and to make him a knight in honour of his services to Queen and country.

Mendoza wrote that, as Elizabeth picked up the sword to tap Drake on the shoulder in the traditional knighting ceremony, she said that she was going to cut his head off. It was just a joke, only it **must have seemed** in very poor taste to Drake because, in those days, kings and queens sometimes did decapitate people who displeased them! Joking aside, she gladly accepted the treasure, including a brooch in the shape of a frog made of diamonds.

That night there was a great celebration on the ship with the banquet which Mendoza described as being "finer than **has ever been seen** in England". A large crowd had gathered on a wooden bridge connecting the ship to the shore to watch the festivities. They cheered when the banquet ended with a toast to the new knight, Sir Francis Drake "the master thief of the unknown world".

But English pride **was suddenly punctured** when the bridge **collapsed**, plunging about a hundred of Queen Elizabeth's loyal subjects into the water. Fortunately, no one **drowned** but the collapse certainly **put** a dampener on the glorious occasion.

And a few years later the warnings of the Queen's advisers **would be vindicated** when war broke out between England and Spain.

Questions

A. The verb **had just returned** appears in the very first sentence of this story. Does it express **(1)** something that happened at a definite time in the past which was finished or does it refer to **(5)** something in the past that happened before something else in the past?

B. When the Queen's advisers told her she **would** risk war with Spain, does the verb **would** refer to **(6)** a past habit or something that happened regularly or often in the past or does it refer to **(7)** something that was still in the future?

C. Look at the verbs **were watching** and **would** in paragraph three. Which one **(3)** describes something that was still in progress, in other words, unfinished, and which one describes **(7)** something that was still in the future?

D. Was Drake's reaction to the Queen's joke about cutting off his head **(1)** something that happened at a definite time in the past and was finished or **(8)** speculation about the past.

E. When Mendoza described the banquet as being "finer than **has ever been seen** in England" was he referring **(1)** to something that happened at a definite time in the past and was finished or **(4)** to unspecified or indefinite times in the past, in other words, general experience?

F. Which is the correct way to put Mendoza's comment in **(10)** indirect speech:

Mendoza **said** the banquet **is** finer that **has ever been seen** in England

OR

Mendoza **said** the banquet **was** finer than **had ever been seen** in England

G. Was the puncturing of English pride **(1)** something that happened at a definite time in the past and was finished at that time or **(3)** something that was still in progress, in other words, unfinished?

H. Was the collapse of the bridge **(1)** something that happened at a definite time in the past and was finished at that time or **(3)** something that was still in progress, in other words, unfinished?

I. Were the facts that no one **drowned** and that a dampener was **put** on the occasion **(1)** things that happened at a definite time in the past and were finished or **(3)** things that were still in progress, in other words, unfinished?

J. Was that fact the Queen's advisers turned out to be right **(1)** something that happened at a definite time in the past and was finished or **(7)** something that, in 1581, was still in the future?

A ... B ... C **(3)** ...... **(7)** ...... D ... E ...
F...
...G ... H ... I ... J ...

Summary

One day in 1581 a great banquet was held on a ship called the *Golden Hind* which was in a harbour near London. The feast was in honour of Francis Drake, one of England's favourite sons, who had just returned from a round-the-world trip with a cargo of fabulous treasure, said to be worth billions in today's currency. Drake **A ...** to give the treasure to the Queen although her closest counsellors **B ...** her not to accept the gift because the treasure had been plundered from Spanish ships. If she accepted the treasure, it **C ......** to trouble with Spain, possibly war. The Queen ignored the advice. She accepted the gift of the treasure, made Drake a knight and organised the great banquet to celebrate. A crowd gathered on a bridge connecting the ship to the shore to watch proceedings. Unfortunately, the bridge suddenly collapsed and they all fell into the water. Fortunately, no one drowned. But the outlook was not so bright for relations between England and Spain. Within a few years, as the Queen's advisers **D ...**, they **E ......** at war.

(1) advised (3) was planning (5) had predicted (7) would lead (7) would be

Famous writer pilloried (C1)

Daniel Defoe, who **lived** three hundred years ago, is best known today for writing one of the most famous novels in the English language, *Robinson Crusoe* which is about the adventures of a man who was shipwrecked on a deserted island.

But long before he achieved fame and fortune as a novelist, Defoe **got** into serious trouble with the British government in 1703 by writing a satirical pamphlet which they did not like. As a result, he **was charged** with libel, put in prison, fined and sentenced to spend some time in the pillory.

The pillory was a particularly nasty form of punishment for people who had committed minor crimes. The aim was to humiliate them. They would be forced to stand in a public place with their necks and wrists locked in a wooden framework so they could not move.

If that was not humiliation enough, people **would** insult them, spit on them and throw things such as eggs and rotten fruit at them, sometimes causing them physical pain as well as emotional distress.

As it happened, Defoe was sentenced to three turns in the pillory. He was also ordered to pay a fine and serve a prison sentence. Of all the punishments, it was the humiliation of the pillory that he feared most.

But he need not have worried. The people of London had a keener sense of justice than the judges who had sentenced him and instead of pelting him with rotten eggs and insults, the public showered him with flowers and drank to his health. They knew that he **had struck** a blow for freedom of speech.

Although the pillory no longer exists, we still use the word, only now it is a verb rather than a noun. To "pillory" someone is to subject them to public ridicule and contempt without physically restraining them. It is a very useful verb to describe what often happens on social media when mobs set out to humiliate someone who has, in some way, caused offence.

Questions

A. When the story says Daniel Defoe **lived** three hundred years ago does it mean **(1)** something that happened at a definite time in the past and was finished or **(2)** a state that existed in the past?

B. When the story says Defoe **got** into trouble does it mean **(1)** something that happened at a definite time in the past and is finished or **(2)** a state that existed in the past?

C. "He **was charged** with libel." Is this **(1)** something that happened at a definite time in the past and was finished or **(2)** a state that existed in the past?

D. When the story says people **would** insult those who were in the pillory, spit on them and throw stuff at them, does it mean that these things **(1)** happened at a definite time in the past and were finished or **(6)** that they were past habits or things that happened regularly or often in the past?

E. The second last paragraph says the public threw flowers at him because he **had struck** a blow for freedom of speech. Does **had struck** express **(1)** something that happened at a particular time in the past and was finished or **(5)** something in the past that happened before something else in the past, in this example the public showering him with flowers and drinking to his health?

A ... B ... C ... D ... E ...

Summary

In 1703 a British journalist called Daniel Defoe **A ...** by the government for publishing something they did not like. As well as a fine and a prison sentence, Defoe was ordered to stand in the pillory. This **B ...** an old-fashioned punishment in which people convicted of crimes **C ......** to stand in a public place with their necks and wrists trapped in a wooden framework. The public **D ......** them, spit at them and throw rotten fruit at them. Naturally, Defoe **E ...** the experience but he was in for a nice surprise. The public were very much on his side in his dispute with the government and instead of rotten fruit, they threw flowers and instead of cursing him, they sang his praises.

(1) was severely punished (2) was (3) was dreading (6)would be forced (6) would abuse

Bearding the lions in their den (C1)

When Peter the Great, Tsar of Russia, **returned** to Moscow from a long tour of Europe in 1698, a large crowd of leading citizens gathered to greet him and pay their respects. All the great and good were there including Alexis Shein, the commander of the army and Prince Fedor Romodanovsky, Governor-General of Moscow who **had been** the effective ruler of Russia in Peter's absence.

Everything went very much as expected at first. There were many fond greetings and embraces as the noblemen paid their respects. But no one realised that Peter had come to beard the lions in their den. This expression is a metaphor that means to confront someone face to face and challenge them.

Only in this case, there was a literal element to it because while everyone **was celebrating**, Peter **did** something shocking and completely unexpected. He took out a razor and began personally shaving the beards off some of the most powerful men in the land.

To get a sense of just how shocking this was, you need to understand the importance of beards in Russian culture and society at the time. As in many other countries, they were symbols of masculine pride and dignity. One of Peter's predecessors, Ivan the Terrible, **had declared** it a sin to shave your beard off and the religious authorities considered beardless men to be shameful and beyond the reach of salvation.

To the assembled dignitaries on that day in 1698, who apparently laughed nervously as Peter went about his work, it **must have seemed** like a random act of madness. But there was a method in Peter's madness. Peter wanted to modernise Russia and to him the beards were symbols of the old traditions that were holding it back and preventing it from embracing innovative technologies and new ways of doing things.

The tour of Europe he **had just been on** was not a holiday or a diplomatic mission, it was a study tour. He had gone with 250 of his countrymen to learn what he could from the shipbuilders, carpenters and mechanics of the west, especially in England and the Netherlands.

He had learned these trades himself and he hoped his subjects **would** do likewise. Another thing he had learned was that most men in the West were clean-shaven and, again, he thought his subjects should follow suit and be just like them. So, he cut their beards off as a symbol of the new policy of progress and modernisation and he followed up by banning beards the length and breadth of the land.

But traditions and cultures die hard, and many men **refused** to comply forcing Peter into a compromise.

"You **can** keep your beards," he said, "but you **will have to** pay a beard tax."

To prove they had paid the tax, men **wore** a medallion showing a picture of a beard and the words "tax paid". But even beard-tax paying men had to be careful if they came face-to-face with the great Tsar. He never really accepted beards and without warning, he was likely to pull out a razor and roughly hack off a man's beard regardless of whether he had paid his taxes.

Questions

A. Was Peter's return to Moscow **(1)** something that happened at a definite time in the past and was finished or **(3)** was it something still in progress, in other words, unfinished?

B. In Peter's absence, Prince Romodanovsky **had been** in charge of Russia. Was this **(1)** something that happened at a definite time in the past and was finished or **(5)** something that happened before Peter's return from Europe?

C. There are two verbs in this sentence: "But while everyone **was celebrating**, Peter **did** something shocking and completely unexpected". Which one describes **(1)** something that happened at a definite time in the past and was finished and which one describes **(3)** something that was still in progress, in other words, unfinished?

D. Peter's predecessor, Ivan the Terrible, **had declared** it a sin for a man to shave his beard off. Did this happen **(1)** at a particular time in the past and was finished or **(5)** before something else in the past, that is, the time that Peter the Great ruled that men should be unshaven.

E. The story says that Peter's action in cutting of the beards of his men **must have seemed** like a random act of madness. Was this **(2)** a state that existed in the past or **(8)** speculation about the past?

F. In the context of this story, was Peter's tour **(1)** something that happened at a definite time in the past and was finished or **(5)** something that had happened before something else in the past, his campaign to modernise Russia, which it still affected in some way?

G. When Peter said he hoped that his subjects **would** learn trades and crafts, was this something **(1)** that happened at a definite time in the past and was finished or **(7)** something that was still in the future?

107

H. Not all men obeyed Peter's order to cut off their beards. Was this **(1)** something that happened at a definite tie in the past and was finished or **(7)** something that was still in the future?

I. Peter is quoted directly as saying "You **can** keep your beards but you **will have to** pay a beard tax." Which is the correct way to put this quote in **(10)** indirect or reported speech:

They **can** keep their beards, he **said**, but they **will have to** pay a beard tax

or

They **could** keep their beards, he **said**, but they **would have to** pay a beard tax.

J. The story says men **wore** medallions to prove they had paid the beard tax. Was this **(1)** something that happened at a definite time in the past and was finished or **(6)** a past habit or something that happened regularly or often in the past?

A ... **B** ... **C (1)** ... **(3)** ... **D** ... **E** ... **F** ... **G** ... **H** ... **I**...
.... **J** ...

Summary

One day, back in the seventeenth century, the Tsar of Russia, Peter the Great, **A** ... from a trip to Western Europe and did something very strange. He started to shave the beards off the most powerful men in his cabinet. It **B** ... crazy to his people but there was a method to his madness. Peter **C** ... his country to become modern and he had visited Europe to try to find out the secrets of the Europeans' economic and technological success. Among other things, he **D** ... that European men tended to be clean-shaven in contrast to the men of Russia. So, he decided that all the men of Russia should shave. The problem was that the Russians rather liked their beards and many refused to do as he asked. In the end, Peter was forced to compromise.

He told the men they could keep their beards but they **E ...** have to pay a tax for the privilege.

(1) returned (2) wanted (5) had noticed (7) would (8) must have seemed

The haves and the have-nots (C1)

It is a lamentable fact in the world of humans that some people have more than their fair share of good looks, brains and money while others must do with less. The former group are known informally as "the haves" and the latter "the have-nots". A corollary to this dismal state of affairs is that the haves get all the excitement and glory while the have-nots do the drudge work that is essential for success or, if the task be warfare, eventual victory, without much more than a "thank you, now get back to work".

It is much the same in the world of animals. Just look at the difference in status between the horse and the mule. Can you think of a famous mule today? Probably not, but you shouldn't be too hard pressed to think of a famous horse. All you need to do is turn to the racetrack or, indeed, to the history books which are populated with famous, and glamorous horses: Bucephalus **was** Alexander the Great's horse, Marengo (Napoleon), Traveller (General Robert E. Lee), Seabiscuit and Phar Lap (famous racehorses) and many others including film and television stars such as Hopalong Cassidy's horse, Trigger, the Lone Ranger's Silver and Mr Ed, a horse who could apparently speak English.

But mules? It's not just that **they've gone out** of fashion, they were never in fashion. They **have always been** the have-nots compared to the glamorous haves listed above. One of the best descriptions of the position of the mule in history is to be found in John D. Billings' *Hardtack and Coffee*, a memoir of his time in the Union Army during the American Civil War.

Billings tells us the mules were the drudges of the war. They used to carry the baggage: the food, the ammunition, the mobile field kitchens, what in modern-day parlance would be called "logistics". Many knowledgeable people at the time thought the North could not have won the war without their mule trains keeping the soldiers fed and stocked up with ammunition.

One big advantage the mules had over horses was that they were much tougher. They could handle rough ground and they were not too particular about their diet. In fact, Billings tells us, a mule once ate his driver's great coat.

The question naturally arises that if they were so hardy and low maintenance, why were they not used for the glamour roles with the calvary and the artillery? The answer, according to Billings, was not so much a matter of appearances as personality. Mules, like many men, **preferred** to do their bit for the war effort away from the front lines. Under fire mules **were** likely to panic and create a stir whereas horses were more stoic, they **handled** the pressure better. And, importantly, they **were** much more willing and obedient than the mules who **had** a justified reputation for being stubborn and going on strike and quick to kick if they were displeased.

Billings observed some mules in the Confederate Army withdrawing under fire near the end of the war and they **became** so unmanageable that the mule drivers had to turn them loose leading to further chaos in the ranks of the retreating army. No wonder the handsome, calmer, braver and more obedient horses got the glory jobs with the cavalry and the artillery!

But on one occasion, the mules won their share of glory as well even if it was only a footnote in history. It **occurred** on the night of 28 October 1863 when Confederate forces **were attacking** a Union position at Wauhatchie in Tennessee.

It just so happened that 200 Union mules were close by and, as expected, they **became** highly agitated at the sound of gunfire and the smell of gunpowder in the dark. The Union mule handlers **were spooked** and thinking their position was about to be overrun did as the Confederates **would** do three years later and set their mules free.

In their panic, the mules **stampeded** towards the Confederates who, in the dark, took them to be Union cavalry and they, in turn, **panicked** and **fled**.

One Union officer **was so impressed** with the story that he said, "those mules outta be promoted to horses," using the colloquial word "outta" which means "ought to" or "should".

And Ambrose Bierce, a famous journalist and short story writer of the day, **immortalised** the mules of Wauhatchie in "Jupiter Doke, Brigadier General". The story tells of how an incompetent amateur general has his reputation saved when a herd of panicking mules charges enemy lines and is mistaken for Union cavalry.

Questions

A. The story says Bucephalus **was** Alexander the Great's horse. Is this a reference **(1)** to something that happened at a definite time in the past and was finished or **(2)** to a state that existed in the past?

B. Look at this quote from the story: "It's not just that **they've gone out** of fashion, they were never in fashion. They **have always been** the have-nots". Are these verbs referring to **(1)** things that happened at a definite time in the past and were finished or **(4)** things that existed at an unspecified or indefinite time in the past but which, in some ways, still affect the present?

C. Billings' explanation for why mules were not used on the front line has the following verbs **were**, **preferred**, **handled** and **had**. Are these verbs **(1)** expressing things that happened at a particular time in the past and were finished or **(2)** expressing states that existed in the past?

D. Billings observed some mules near the end of the war and they **became** unmanageable. Was this **(1)** something that happened at a definite time in the past and was finished or **(2)** a state that existed in the past?

E. Look at this quote from the story "It **occurred** on the night of 28 October 1863 when Confederate forces **were attacking** a Union position at Wauhatchie in Tennessee". Which of these verbs **(1)** expresses something that happened at a definite time in the past and was finished and which one **(3)** expresses something that was still in progress, in other words, unfinished?

F. At the sound of gunfire the mules **became** highly agitated, and their handlers **were spooked**. Are these verbs expressing **(1)** things that happened at a definite time in the past and were finished or **(2)** states that existed in the past?

G. The mule handlers did what the Confederates **would** do at the end of the war. Does the verb **would** in this context express **(6)** a past habit or something that happened regularly or often in the past, **(7)** something that was still in the future t the time of the battle, **(8)** speculation about the past or **(9)** something that did not happen, something hypothetical, unreal or imaginary?

H. The mules **stampeded** and the Confederates **panicked** and **fled**. Are these things **(1)** that happened at a definite time and the past and were finished or **(2)** are they states that existed in the past or **(3)** are they things that were still in progress, in other words, unfinished?

114

I. One officer **was so impressed** with the story that he said the mules "outta" (or should) be promoted to horses. Is that something **(1)** that happened at a definite time in the past and was finished of **(2)** was it a state that existed in the past?

J. Ambrose Bierce **immortalised** the mules of Wauhatchie. Is this **(1)** something that he did at a definite time in the past and was finished of **(2)** was it a state that existed in the past?

A … B … C … D … E (1) …… (3) …… F … G … H … I… J…

Summary

Many strange and extraordinary things **A …** in the history of warfare but perhaps none stranger that what occurred during the Battle of Wauhatchie in the American Civil War. It happened in October 1863, soon after the war **B ……**, when a force of Confederate soldiers **C …** a Union position at Wauhatchie in Tennessee. Tethered nearby were 200 mules that the Union Army **D ……** to transport supplies and ammunition. At nightfall, the mules were panicking because of the noise of battle and their handlers set them free. In their fright, the mules **E …** towards the Confederate lines. In the darkness, the Confederates mistook the mules for charging Union cavalry and they, in turn, panicked and fled. One union officer was so impressed that he famously remarked the mules ought to be promoted to horses.

(1) stampeded (3) was attacking (4) have happened (5) had started (5) had been using

Ten ways of talking about the past

Here are the ten basic questions that highlight the meaning of the different ways of talking about the past in English. Each question is followed by an explanation and examples most of which are drawn from the stories in this book. Plus, there are sections on things to watch out for, such as when a verb form can be used with different meanings.

There are two important points to keep in mind. One is that contrasting these questions is one of the best ways to grasp the meaning. For instance, if you are having trouble with **(1)** contrast it with **(3)** and ask yourself what the difference is.

The second point is to notice the context. For instance, the past simple verb **went** could be **(1)**, that is something that happened at a time in the past and was finished. But it could also be **(6)**, something that happened regularly or often. Or it could be **(8)**, speculation about the past.

The way to tell the difference is in the context. The latter two will usually be accompanied by some sort of qualifiers. In **(6)** they will be qualifiers of frequency such as **usually** or **often**. In the case of **(8)** qualifiers indicating speculation such as **possibly**, **probably** or **likely**.

1 Was it an action at a definite time in the past that was finished?

Here is an example from the story "Tragedy plus Time": "In the grey, misty morning … he **woke up** and **decided** to greet the dawn with a tune on his pipes." The answer to question **(1)** is yes. It happened at a definite time – the morning – and the actions were clearly completed or finished at that time.

To express this meaning, you need to use a form of the verb known as the **past simple** which is usually made by adding **-ed** to the basic form of the verb: decide / **decided**, arrive / **arrived**, change / **changed** and so on. There are, of course, many exceptions to this basic rule hear / **heard**, take / **took**, sleep / **slept**, write / **wrote**, become / **became**. You should learn these because the past simple is the most common way to talk about the past in English. It is used to tell stories and to relate everyday events in your life.

It is worth repeating and stressing the two key points. The first is that when we use the past simple, we are talking about a definite time in the past and this is nearly always stated explicitly, as it is in the example above, or, if not, the time is obvious from the context. The second is that the action or event was finished.

Questions and negatives

To make questions and negatives in the past simple use the past simple forms of the auxiliary verbs **be** and **do**: **was/were**, **did**. For example:

When **did** he wake up?

He **didn't** wake up until 10 o'clock.

Watch out for …

The past simple is also used for **(2)** states that existed in the past, **(6)** past habits and repeated actions when combined with adverbs of frequency such as **every**, **usually**, **often** and

118

regularly and **(8)** speculation about the past when combined with adverbs such as **possibly**, **probably** and **likely**. In indirect or reported speech the past simple replaces the present simple, see **(10)** below.

2 Was it a state that existed in the past?

You also use the **past simple** to talk about states that existed in the past as opposed to events or things people did. States are existing, being, having, possessing, knowing, feeling, opinions and abilities.

This example comes from "Scared out of their wits": "They **were so worried** that they slept with their candles alight that night." The first part of the sentence does not express something that they did, rather it describes the state they were in, what they were feeling: worry. But apart from that, the rules are the same as for **(1)**. There is a specific time reference – "**that night**" – and the state is finished.

An important pattern to notice is that state verbs and action verbs are often used in combination, the state verb providing the background or context to the action. This example comes from "The diamond sting": "Surprising as it may seem, she **was** right. She **was**, indeed, a direct descendant of Henry II, the last king of the Valois dynasty and, after her father's death, through a series of lucky breaks plus sheer willpower, she **managed** to put her case to King Louis XIV who **granted** her a royal pension."

Ask yourself which of these highlighted verbs express **(1)** something that was done and finished at a definite time in the past and which ones express **(2)** states that existed in the past? The first two verbs are examples of **(2)**. They express the states of being and knowing – she **was** right, she **was** a descendent of Henry II.

These states provide the background and the context to the specific actions: she **managed** to put her case and Louis **granted** her a pension which are examples of **(1)**. Each of them performed an action at a definite time in the past which was finished.

Watch out for ...

You can also express finished states in the past with **used to + infinitive**. For example, "Juan Carlos **used to** be the king of Spain."

Used to + infinitive can also express habits and repeated or regular actions in the past see question **(6)** below. And it also means "accustomed to" in the present tense. For example, "I am **used to** getting up early". The pattern here is different however, it is **used to + -ing verb**.

3 Was it something unfinished or in progress in the past?

In the examples above the states and actions being expressed are finished. But sometimes you need to refer to states and actions in the past that were not finished at the time or, to put it another way, were still in progress. You do this by using the form known as the **past progressive** or **past continuous** which is made by combining the past-simple form of the verb **be** with an **-ing verb**: **was / were + -ing verb**.

This example is from "Scared out of their wits": "Whoever it was, **was pacing** back and forth across the floor." To get the meaning of this sentence ask yourself **(1)** if this was an action at a definite time in the past and was finished or **(3)** if it was still in progress, in other words, unfinished? The answer is **(3)**, the action was happening, or in progress. It was not yet finished at the time we are talking about.

There are two very common patterns using the past progressive. The first is when you need to describe an action in progress that is interrupted by another action which was then finished. To do this you need to use the past progressive form and the past simple together. This example comes from "A formidable woman": "They **were hunting** in the Highlands when the war **began**." There are two verbs in this sentence. Ask yourself **(1)** which one expresses an action at a definite time in the past that was finished and **(3)** which one expresses something that was still in progress, in other words, unfinished? The answers are **(1) began** and **(3) were hunting**.

The second pattern is when you want to describe two or more things happening at the same time and which were unfinished

122

at the time you are referring to. This example comes from the story "Brushes with Death": "He **was sitting up** in bed, **smoking** a cigar and **giving** advice on how to handle the Great Depression, the economic crisis that **was worrying** the whole world at the time." Ask yourself **(1)** did each of these things happen at a definite time in the past and were finished or **(3)** were they all still in progress, in other words, unfinished? The answer is **(3)**. In this sentence you have a series of actions and states that existed or were happening at the same time, none of them were finished. The pattern is obvious: **past progressive + past progressive**. In the example above there are four verbs in the past progressive for the three actions – **was sitting up**, **[was] smoking**, **[was] giving** – and one state – **was worrying** – that existed or happened at the same time.

Negatives and questions

To make negatives you simply insert **not**: Whoever it was, **was not pacing** back and forth across the floor.

And for questions **was not / wasn't** or **were not / weren't +
-ing form of the verb**: **Wasn't he pacing** back and forth across the floor? / **Was he pacing** back and for across the floor?

Watch out for ...

Many state verbs do not take progressive forms.

Other ways of talking about the past, **(4)** the present perfect and **(5)** the past perfect, also have progressive forms. The meaning is that same as with the past continuous, to express an action or state that existed or was in progress and, most importantly, was unfinished at the time you are referring to.

Also note that in reported speech **(10)**, the past continuous is used instead of the present continuous.

4 Was it something at an unspecified or indefinite time in the past that still affects the present?

Sometimes you need to refer to things in the past that are still connected in some way to the present as opposed to being finished. To do this you need to use a verb form known as the **present perfect** which is **has / have + past participle**. People are often confused by the name of this form because it contains the word "present" when it is referring to the past which seems like a contradiction. But it is a good way to remind yourself that this is about the past that has a bearing on the present. And you should note also that it uses the present tense of the verb **have** combined with the past participle.

You can use this form in three slightly different ways: to refer to the recent past, to refer to something that existed for a period in the past and, finally, to refer to a general experience from the past without a specific time reference.

First, the recent past. When something is very recent it is usually easier to see its effects on the present. Here is an example from "Brushes with Death", the story about the British Second World War Prime Minister, Winston Churchill being knocked down by a car in New York and badly injured. As he lay on the road, he thought to himself: "I **have been** run over by a motor car in America …" To clarify the meaning, ask yourself **(1)** did this happen at a definite time in the past and was finished or **(4)** was it something from Churchill's recent past which in some way affected his present, while he was lying on the road? The answer is **(4)** and the full context makes the point even clearer when he goes on to describe the great pain he was feeling from his injuries.

124

To emphasise that something has happened very recently, and to prevent ambiguity, you can use **just**. For instance, Churchill could have said: "I have **just** been run over …" Other words you can use to emphasise that you are talking about recent things and not things that existed in the distant past, are **already**, **still**, and **yet**.

I have **already** done that. (This means you finished sooner than you expected.)

We **still** have not completed our task. (Used in negatives to mean taking longer than you expected.)

I haven't finished **yet**. (Used in negatives and questions to mean up to this time or moment.)

The second use of the present perfect is to express something that began in the past, or existed in the past, and continued for a period and still affects the present. This often done with **for**, to express the period that it has been going on, or **since** to pinpoint the moment that it began. This example comes from "A nice cuppa", the story about how England became a nation of tea drinkers: "While tea drinking **has increased** in England **since** Catherine's day, it **has decreased** in Portugal." Were these **(1)** things that happened at a definite time in the past and were finished or **(4)** things that began in Catherine's day and which still affect the present? The answer is **(4)**, England is still a nation of tea drinkers while Portugal prefers coffee.

Or you could put it this way: "England **has been** a nation of tea drinkers **for** 300 hundred years." Was this **(1)** something that happened at a definite time in the past and was finished or **(4)** was it something that happened over a period of many years and which still affects the present? The answer is **(4)**. The important difference between this example and the previous one is that it uses **has + past participle + for** to refer to a period (300 years) and the previous one uses **has** + **past participle** + **since** to refer to a point in time (the time when Catherine was Queen).

Finally, you use the present perfect to refer to something from the past with no time reference but which affects the present because it is part of general experience. Here is another example from "Brushes with Death". Churchill describes looking for the house of an old friend in New York, just before his accident: "I **have been** there before and I'm sure I'll recognise it." To clarify the meaning, contrast the present perfect with the past simple. Was Churchill's visit to the house **(1)** something that happened at a definite time in the past and was finished or **(4)** did this happen at some indefinite or non-specific time in the past and which was part of his general experience and therefore had some bearing on the present? The answer is **(4)**.

Because the present perfect is used in this way to refer to experience throughout your whole life or all time, it is often combined with the adverbs **ever**, meaning "any time" and **never**, meaning "at no time".

Ever is used in questions: "Have you **ever** been there?" Is the questioner asking **(1)** whether you went there at one definite time in the past or **(4)** whether you have been there at any time in your life, whether it is part of your general experience? The answer is **(4)**.

Never is used in negatives: "No, I've **never** been there." Is the reply **(1)** that you were not there at a definite time in the past which is now finished or **(4)** that you were not there at any time in your life, that it forms no part of your general experience? Again, the answer is **(4)**.

Watch out for ...

You can emphasise that something has been in progress up to the present time by combining the present perfect with a verb

126

ending in **-ing**, **has/have** + **past participle** + **-ing verb**: "The English **have been drinking** tea **for** more than 300 years." OR "The English **have been drinking** tea **since** the seventeenth century." Ask yourself **(1)** is this something that happened at a definite time in the past and is now finished or **(4)** is it something that was in progress, or unfinished, in the past and affects the present because it is still happening? The answer is **(4)**.

Also note that in reported speech **(10)**, the past perfect replaces the present perfect.

5 Was it something in the past that affected something else in the past?

This is very like the present perfect except that the past event or state affects another point in the past rather than the present. For example, take this sentence from the story "The last laugh", the scene is a dinner party in London in the 1660s where the guests are discussing King Louis XIV of France: "The guests praised Louis for the way he **had raised** his kingdom and himself to greatness." Was the fact that Louis **had raised** his kingdom to greatness **(1)** something that happened at a definite time in the past and was finished or **(5)** something that happened before something else in the past – the dinner party – which it affected? The answer is **(5)**. Clearly, Louis and his kingdom rose to greatness first and this affected the moment in the past at which the dinner party took place because the guests were talking about him.

To express this idea, you use a form of the verb known as the **past perfect**: **had + past participle**. Notice that it differs from the present perfect because it uses the past tense of the verb **have** instead of the present. Apart from this very important distinction, the past perfect, like the present perfect, can be combined with **just**, **already**, **for**, **since**, **ever** and **never**. The past perfect can also be used without time references to indicate experience and combined with an **-ing verb** to make a continuous form.

Watch out for …

It is okay to use the past simple instead of the past perfect when the context makes it perfectly clear which thing happened first: "The army **won** the battle just after they **[had] crossed** the river." Both verbs in this sentence are past simple but the action that happened first was the crossing of the river. Prepositions that express time, such as **after** and **before**, are used to make clear the order in which things happened.

You can also use the past continuous instead of the past perfect continuous if the meaning is obvious.

Also, the past perfect form – **had + past participle** – is part of the pattern known as the third conditional which is a way of expressing hypothetical or unreal things in the past, see **(9)** below.

And, finally, note that the past perfect verb form does not change when direct speech is changed to reported speech. See **(10)** below.

6 Was it a past habit or something that happened regularly or often?

There are three ways of talking about past habits: The **past simple + adverbs of frequency**, **used to + infinitive** and, finally, using the modal auxiliary **would**. Context is especially important here to avoid confusion because the **past simple**, **used to** and **would** all have other meanings as well.

The best clues to watch out for in the context are adverbs and expressions indicating frequency and the duration of time. These tell you that the meaning is a repeated action or habit over a period rather than just one act at one time. Keep an eye out for words and phrases such as: **always**, **usually**, **often**, **regularly**, **frequently**, **sometimes**, **daily**, **hourly**, **monthly**, **every (day, week, month etc)** or expressions such as **throughout**, **during**, **once an hour (a day, a week etc)** or **twice a day (an hour, a week etc)**.

Past simple + adverb of frequency

Here is an example from the story "Tragedy plus Time": "Some people were appointed as body collectors to go through the streets **every night** to collect corpses which they **carried** on "dead carts" to a place of mass burials." Was it **(1)** something that happened at a definite time in the past and was finished or **(6)** a past habit or something that happened regularly or often in the past? In this example the phrase **every night** is the clue that tells you the past simple verb **carried** in this context means **(6)** something that happened regularly rather than just once.

Used to + infinitive

This example comes from "A nice cuppa": "Ordinary people **used to drink** ale and coffee." Was it **(2)** a state that existed in the past and was finished or **(6)** or was it a past habit or something that happened regularly or often in the past? Again, the answer is **(6)**. The broader context of the story makes it clear that it is referring to a habit rather than something that just happened once. **Used to** does not need a reference to frequency or duration. But you could use these expressions for emphasis or clarity: "Ordinary people **always** / **nearly always** / **often** / **frequently** used to drink ale or coffee."

Would

This example comes from the story "Too Good to be True": "When someone, usually a company, sent correspondence internationally they **would** include the cost of the postage for the reply." Was it **(1)** something that happened at a definite time in the past and was finished or **(6)** a past habit or something that happened regularly or often in the past? The answer is **(6)**. Again, the context of the story makes it clear that this was standard practice at the time. As with **used to**, references to frequency are not necessary but you can use them for emphasis. For instance, you could say: "They would **always** / **usually** include the cost of postage ..."

Watch out for ...

Would has many other meanings. It is used as the past form of **will** to talk about and predict the future from the perspective of the past **(7)**, it is used to speculate about what might or might not have happened or existed in the past **(8)** and it is used in the third conditionals to talk about hypothetical or unreal things in the past **(9)**. And don't forget that the past simple is also used for **(1)** things that happened at definite times in the past and were finished and **used to** is also used for **(2)** states that existed in the past.

7 Was it still in the future?

This is often called "the future in the past" which seems like a contradiction but it is not. It is a way of talking about the future from a point of view in the past. First you look back to a point in time in the past, then you look forward to the future from that point. Here is an example from "A nice cuppa", describing how Portuguese Princess, Catherine of Braganza, arrived in England in 1662: "Catherine **went on to** marry King Charles." Was the marriage **(1)** something that happened at a particular time in the past and was finished or **(7)** was it something that had not yet happened at a definite time in the past but was still in the future? The answer is **(7)**. In 1662 she had not yet married Charles but she would marry him in the future. **Went on to** and **would** are two of the most common ways of expressing this idea but there are others: **was to / were to, was going to / were going to** and **would go on to**.

These phrases are very common in histories, biographies and other forms of non-fiction writing when the authors know what lay in the future from the perspective of the times they are writing about. But sometimes you need to talk about the future in the past when someone in the past is predicting or promising something. No one can ever be one hundred per certain about the future so often these predictions, prophecies and promises do not come true.

Take, for example, this sentence about Richard Brothers a famous prophet of doom in 1790s London: "He prophesied that, at a specific time in January 1791, the city of London **was going to be** destroyed." Clearly, he said this in the past but he was talking about the future. Fortunately, his prophecy did not come true. To clarify the meaning ask yourself: was the destruction of London **(1)** something that happened at a definite time in the past and was finished or **(7)** something that was predicted at a particular time in the past but, in fact, never happened? The answer is **(7)**.

Watch out for ...

Would here is used as the past form of **will** but as a modal verb it has a number of different uses when talking about the past see, above, **(6)** past habits and below, **(8)** past speculation and **(9)** hypothetical past.

When direct speech is changed to reported speech, **will** becomes **would**. See **(10)** below.

8 Is it speculation about the past?

If you are not sure about something in the past, you can speculate about what you think is true by using a modal verb **(would/could/may/might/must/should, ought to) + have + past participle**. For example, this sentence from "Punctured pride": "It was just a joke, only it **must have seemed** in very poor taste to Drake." Was Drake's reaction **(2)** a state that existed in the past or **(8)** something that the author thinks was true but cannot be certain about, in other words speculation? The answer is **(8)**.

Another example, this one from "Off to a bad start": "They **probably would have made** him think that his original instinct was the right one." This example uses **would** and reinforces the idea that the author is not 100 per cent sure by adding **probably**. Check the meaning by asking whether this was **(6)** a past habit or something that happened regularly or often in the past, **(7)** something that was still in the future from the perspective of a definite time in the past or **(8)** speculation about the past? The answer is **(8)**.

You can also use the past simple with words like **probably**, **possibly**, **likely** or **unlikely** to express what you think was true in the past but cannot be absolutely certain: "It was just a joke but it **probably was not** very funny to Drake." Was this **(1)** something that existed at a definite time in the past or **(8)** speculation about the past? The answer is **(8)**.

9 Was it something hypothetical or unreal in the past?

In the examples above, the author believes the statements are true but cannot be certain. But sometimes you will need to express something that you know was not true, in other words something hypothetical, unreal or imaginary in the past. You do this by using exactly the same pattern to the one above: **modal verb (would/could/may/might/should, ought to) + have + past participle**.

This example comes from "Too good to be true" in which confidence trickster Charles Ponzi imagines defrauding the Soviet Union out of billions of dollars: "'What a joke on the communists that **would have been**,' he said." Was this **(8)** something that the author thinks is true but cannot be certain about, in other words speculation or **(9)** something that did not happen, in other words was just hypothetical, unreal or imaginary? The answer is, of course **(9)**.

One of the most common uses of this form of the verb is in a structure, or pattern, known as the **third conditional** in which you express a hypothetical condition with a hypothetical consequence. The basic pattern is this: **if + past perfect + modal verb (could/would/might/may/should) + have + past participle**.

For example, look at this sentence referring to Adolf Hitler in the story "Brushes with Death": "It is possible that **if Hitler had died**, there **would not have been** a Second World War." There are two parts to this pattern. The first part, known as the conditional clause **if Hitler had died (if + past perfect)** and the second, the consequence clause **there would not have been (modal verb + have + past participle)**. You can change the order if you want to: "It is possible there would not have been a

135

Second World War if Hitler had died." This example is a classic third conditional in which the hypothetical condition and the hypothetical consequence are both in the past. To clarify the meaning ask yourself was this **(1)** something that happened at a definite time in the past and is now finished or **(9)** something hypothetical, unreal or imaginary with a hypothetical consequence in the past? The answer is **(9)**

But often you will need to express a hypothetical condition in the past with hypothetical present consequences. To do this you replace the consequence clause with **modal (would, could, might, may, should, ought to) + basic verb**: "If he had died, the world **would be** very different today" or "The world **would be** very different today if he had died." To clarify the meaning ask yourself was this **(1)** something that happened at a definite time in the past and is now finished or **(9)** something hypothetical, unreal or imaginary with a hypothetical consequence in the present? Again, the answer is **(9)**.

Watch out for …

The conditional clauses usually begin with **if**, but not always. They can also begin with **unless**, **provided that**, **as long as** or **on condition that**.

Should/ought to + have + past participle means an obligation that was not fulfilled. This example comes from "Punctured pride": "She **should have listened** to her advisers." Was this **(8)** something the author thinks was true but cannot be certain about or **(9)** something hypothetical, unreal or imaginary? The answer is **(9)** it did not happen, she did not listen to her advisers.

One very tricky aspect of third conditionals is that, because they are referring to unreal or hypothetical things, they reverse the meanings of positive and negative verbs. For example, "**If I hadn't robbed** the bank, I **wouldn't have been** in prison". Ask yourself, did he rob the bank? The answer is yes, he did, even though the verb is negative. And was he in prison? Again, the answer is yes even though the verb is negative.

Now look at this example with positive verbs: "**If I had robbed** the bank, I **would have been** in prison." Again, ask did he rob the bank? This time the answer is no, even though the verb is positive. And was he in prison? Again, the verb is positive but the answer is no.

This is especially tricky when you mix positive and negative verbs in third conditional patterns. For example: "**If I hadn't robbed** the bank, I **would have been** free to celebrate my birthday today." Did he rob the bank? Yes. Was he free on his birthday? No. Now here is another example with the positive verb in the if clause: "**If I had robbed** the bank, I **wouldn't have any** money worries today". Did he rob the bank? No. Does he have money troubles? Yes.

Now look at this authentic example from the story "Brushes with death" which tells the story of how the two most prominent leaders of the Second World War were nearly killed in separate road accidents years before the war broke out: "It is possible that **if Hitler had died**, there **would not have been** a Second World War. Equally, it is possible that, **if Churchill had been killed**, Great Britain **would have surrendered** in 1939".

Did Hitler die? No. Was there a Second World War? Yes. Was Churchill killed? No. Did Britain surrender in 1939? No.

10 Was it something somebody said in the past?

When you summarise what someone said you need to put their statement in the past. This is called reported speech or indirect speech. Here is a quote from the story "A formidable woman": "She wrote 'I **am** lovesick, homesick … and now seasick'." To put this in indirect speech you change the **present simple** verb to the **past simple**: She wrote that she **was** lovesick, homesick … and now seasick.

If the direct speech verb is in the **past simple**, then the indirect verb must be in the **past perfect**. This example comes from "Prophet of Doom": "'I **prayed** to God and asked him to give you sinners another chance,' he said." In indirect speech that would be: He said he **had prayed** to God.

If the verb in direct speech is in the **present perfect** form, you change it to the **past perfect** in indirect speech. "I **have been** run over by a motor car in America" becomes: He said he **had been** run over by a motor car in America.

However, if the verb in direct speech is already in the past perfect, it does not change in reported speech. For example, "I knew my way because I **had been** there before" in reported speech becomes: He **said** he knew his way because he **had been** there before.

Progressive forms follow the same pattern: **present progressive – past progressive, present perfect progressive – past perfect progressive, past progressive – past perfect progressive** and, of course, **past perfect progressive** remains **past perfect progressive**.

Modals **will/can/may** and **shall** become **would/ could/ might** and **should**. For example, this quotation from the film *Monty Python and the Holy Grail*, appears in the story "Tragedy plus Time": "But I'm not dead yet," says the old man to the carter to which the son responds, 'Yes, he is … well, he will be soon, he's very ill'." To put that in reported speech you change the present simple **I'm (I am)** to the past simple and the modal auxiliary **will** to **would**: The old man said he **was** not dead yet but the son said he **would** be soon because he was very ill.

Watch out for …

To avoid conveying the wrong meaning, it is often better to leave verbs expressing opinions and beliefs in the present simple. For instance: "'I **believe** in God,' said the man." If you follow the rule and change this to indirect speech with the present tense verb in the past, you change the meaning: He said he **believed** in God. The direct speech makes it clear that the belief is something that exists in the present, the second sounds as though the man used to believe in God but no longer believes. To make the original meaning clear in indirect speech you should break the rule and keep the verb in the present: He said he **believes** in God.

Answers

Off to a bad start

A (1) was taken (3) was lying B (1) C (5) D (8) E (7)

Summary

A (1) B (2) C (5) D (3) E (7)

Brushes with death

A (8) B (7) C (1) D (1) noticed, rammed, pushed (2) was (3)were travelling, was sitting E (5) F (4) G (10) Churchill thought he **had been** there before and he **was** sure he would recognise it. H (7) I (6) J (9)

Summary

A (3) B (1) C (8) D (7) E (9)

A nice cuppa

A (1) arrived, came (2) wanted B (5) C (4) D (6) E (1) F (7) G (1) H (5) I (4) J (9)

Summary

A (2) B (1) C (8) D (6) E (4)

A formidable woman

A (1) B (1) began (3) were hunting C (2) was (3) were staying D (7) E (10) Hermione **said** she **was** lovesick, homesick … and now seasick F (5) G (6) H (9) I (5) J (7)

Summary

A (5) B (3) C (10) D (1) E (7)

First impressions

A (1) decided (2) was (3) were getting B (6) C (2) D (1) held, did not solve, rejected, asked (2) was, shared E (1)

Summary

A (1) B (3) C (2) D(7) E (8)

The last laugh

A (1) B (1) C (5) D (9) E (1) F (3) G (1) H (3) I (1) heard (2)felt J (4)

Summary

A (6) B (2) C (5) D (1) E (3)

Prophet of doom

A (1) B (3) were looking (5) had lost C (7) D (1) sought (5)had done E (7) F (3) G (9) H (9) I (1) J (10)

Summary

A (7) B (2) C (3) D (4) E (9)

Tragedy plus time

A (4) B (8) C (1) were appointed (3) were dying D (6) E (6) F (8) G (9) H (10) I (1) J (9)

Summary

A (6) would B (6) were loaded C (1) D (3) E (5)

Too good to be true

A (6) B (7) C (3) were gathering (7) would D (2) was prepared (8) must have been E (10) F (6) G (1) began (3) was going H (2) I (2) J (9)

Summary

A (3) B (6) C (7) D (5) E (4)

Scared out of their wits

A (2) B (1) decided, sent, arrived, occupied (2) consisted of, was C (6) D (3) E (1) changed, heard (3) was pacing F (5) G(1)were thrown (3) were sleeping (6) always started H (5) had attacked (7) would I (9) J (2) was (5) had worked.

Summary

A (1) B (8) C (5) D (6) E (7)

Raise your glasses

A (4) B (6) C (1) D (6) E (3) F (4) G (1) made (3) was working H (6) would shout (7) would become I (1) J (9)

Summary

A (2) B (1) C (3) D (7) E (6)

The last straw

Answers A (1) B (2) C (6) D (7) E (9) F (1)

Summary

A (5) B (10) C (1) D (2) E (7)

When royal heads rolled

A (1) established (5) had spent B (1) appointed (2) was (7)would be C (1) was (7) would D (2) E (1)

Summary

A (2) was B (2) was C (1) was executed D (7) E (1) executed

The fruits of his labour

A (1) B (1) C (4) D (4) E (9)

Summary

A (2) B (3) C (1) D (4) has become E (4) have been growing
Nothing new under the sun

A (4) B (4) C (2) D (9) E (1)

Summary

A (4) B (2) C (1) was fined D (9) E (1) recorded
The diamond sting

A (6) B (1) managed, granted (2) was, was C (5) D (7) E (3) F (9) G (1) knelt (3) was trembling H (1) hurried (3) were coming I (5) J (9)

Summary

A (2) B (1) C (5) had insulted D (5) had changed E (7)
Punctured pride

A (5) B (7) C (3) were watching (7) would D (8) E (4) F(10)Mendoza **said** the banquet **was** finer than **had ever been seen** in England G (1) H (1) I (1) J (7)

Summary

A (3) B (1) C (7) would lead D (5) E (7) would be
Famous writer pilloried

A (2) B (1) C (1) D (6) E (5)

Summary

A (1) B (2) C (6) would be forced D (6) would abuse E (3)
Bearding the lions in their den

A (1) B (5) C (1) did (3) was celebrating D (5) E (8) F (5) G(7) H (1) I They **could** keep their beards, he **said**, but they **would have to** pay a beard tax. J (6)

Summary

A (1) B (8) C (2) D (5) E (7)

The haves and the have-nots

A (2) B (4) C (2) D (1) E (1) occurred (3) were attacking F(1) G (7) H (1) I (2) J (1)

Summary

A (4) B (5) had started C (3) D (5) had been using E (1)

Bibliography

Barzun, Jacques, *From Dawn to Decadence*, New York, 2001

Bierce, Ambrose, *The Collected Writings of Ambrose Bierce*, New York, 1963

Billings, John D., *Hardtack and coffee: The unwritten story of army life*, Boston, 1887, Internet Archive, https://tinyurl.com/4a44mhrt

Binns, John *Recollections of the Life of John Binns*, Philadelphia 1854, Internet Archive, https://tinyurl.com/42963wej

'Brief history of Champagne', World of Food and Wine, https://tinyurl.com/43skazmv

Brothers, Richard A., *Revealed Knowledge of the Prophecies and Times*, Springfield, MA, 1797, reprint, Oliver's Bookshelf, https://tinyurl.com/366rsr2p

Carlyle, Thomas, *The French Revolution*, Oxford, 1989

'Champagne and its history', Comité Champagne, https://tinyurl.com/ycx98kr6

Cronin, Vincent, *Louis XIV*, London, 1990

Daily Mail

Doyle, William, *The Oxford History of the French Revolution*, Oxford, 1990

Fraser, Antonia, *King Charles II*, London, 1979

Genuine History of the Good Devil of Woodstock, The, London, 1802 https://tinyurl.com/2nwd5rs9

Gilbert, Martin, *Winston Churchill: The wilderness years,* London, 1981

Gill, N.S., 'Bribery and Cheating at the Ancient Olympics', *ThoughtCo.,* October 2018, https://tinyurl.com/amzzwsk2

Gilliam, Terry and Terry Jones (directors) *Monty Python and the Holy Grail,* Python (Monty) Pictures, 1975

Griffith, Dennis, *Fleet Street: The first 500 years,* London, 2006

'History of Champagne, the truth behind the bubbles', European Waterways website, undated, https://tinyurl.com/2p9mpn3d

Holy Bible, The, Revised Standard Version, London, 1965

Hume, M. Andrew Sharp (ed), 'Calendar of letters and state papers relating to English affairs: preserved principally in the Archives of Simancas: Elizabeth, 1558-[1603]'. Printed for H. M. Stationery Office by Eyre and Spottiswoode. Great Britain. Public Record Office. https://tinyurl.com/v5ezvwkx

Jones, Barry and Meredith V. Dixon, *The MacMillan Dictionary of Biography,* South Melbourne, 1986

Keay, John, *Sowing the Wind: The seeds of conflict in the Middle East,* London, 2003

Kelsey, Harry, *Sir Francis Drake: The Queen's Pirate,* Yale, 1998

Leech, Geoffrey, Benita Cruikshank and Roz Ivanic, *An A-Z of English Grammar & Usage,* Harlow, 2014

Lenman, Bruce P. and Katharine Boyd, *Chambers Dictionary of World History,* Edinburgh, 1993

Lovell, Mary S., *The Churchills,* London, 2011

Mackay, Charles, *Memoirs of Extraordinary Popular Delusions and the Madness of Crowds*, Vol II, 2nd edition, London, 1852

Major, J. Russell, *The Western World: Renaissance to the Present*, 1967, London

Massie, Robert K., *Peter the Great: His life and world*, 1999, London

Milton, Giles, *Samuari William: The adventurer who unlocked Japan*, 2003, London

Morris, Roy, *Ambrose Bierce, Alone in Bad Company*, New York, 1995

New York Herald

New York Times

Nicols, J., *The Progresses and Public Processions of Queen Elizabeth*, vol II, London, 1823

Oldmixon, John, *The History of England During the Reigns of the Royal House of Stuart*, London, 1730, Internet Archive, https://tinyurl.com/ycknsjcb

Pepys, Samuel, *The Diary of Samuel Pepys*, Daily Entries from the 17th Century London Diary, https://www.pepysdiary.com/

Ranfurly, Hermione, Countess of, *To War with Whitaker: The Wartime Diaries of the Countess of Ranfurly*, 1939-1945, 1994

Reresby, Sir John *The Memoirs of the Honourable Sir John Reresby, Bart*, 1735, Oxford Text Archive, Bodleian Library, Oxford University, https://tinyurl.com/mwffvyet

Ridley, Jasper, *Elizabeth I*, London, 1987

Salvemini, Gaetano, *The French Revolution 1788-1792*, London, 1965

Scott, Sir Walter, *Woodstock or the Cavalier*, 1855, Project Gutenberg.org, https://tinyurl.com/2eh2zp89

Scrivener, Jim, *Teaching English Grammar: What to teach and how to teach it*, London, 2010

Shavin, Naomi, 'The Ancient History of Cheating in the Olympics', *Smithsonian Magazine*, 3 August 2016, https://tinyurl.com/yckzdeuv

Shilleto, Arthur Richard (translator), *Pausanias' Description of Greece*, London, 1886, Project Gutenberg, https://tinyurl.com/3mw7a6je

Sinclair, George, *Satan's Invisible World Discovered*, London, 1814, Internet Archive, https://tinyurl.com/yc5sucz3

Stafford Corbett, Julian, *Sir Francis Drake*, London, 1890

Stobart, J.C., *The Glory the was Greece, a survey of Hellenic culture and civilisation*, London, 1933

Sweetman, David, *Gaugin*, London, 1996

Text Inspector, Text Inspector: Analyse the Difficulty Level of English Texts, https//textinspector.com

Thomas, Emory M., *Robert E. Lee*, New York, 1997

Thompson, E.P. *The Making of the English Working Class*, London, 1991

Thompson, J.M., *Robespierre*, Oxford, 1988

Wikipedia

Zuckoff, Mitchell, *Ponzi's Scheme, the true story of a financial legend*, New York, 2006

Grammar index

About the author

During a long career as a journalist, newspaper editor and historian David Hastings always had a secret ambition, to teach English as a foreign language. So, when he retired, he set about achieving this goal. He completed the CELTA (Certificate in English Language Teaching to Adults) course in 2016 and spent four happy years in a language school in Auckland, New Zealand teaching people from all over the world. It was a pleasure to meet and work with them, he said.

Unfortunately, this all ended with the pandemic. New Zealand's borders were closed and students could not come. With plenty of free time on his hands, he decided to do two things. The first was to learn Spanish to gain an understanding of how it feels when you are struggling with a new language, the difficulties you face and, above all, which methods work and which don't. The second was to combine the skills of an editor and writer with those of a language teacher, to produce a series of useful books for people learning English. The first of these was *The Vocabulary Detective* which outlines and demonstrates the all-important skill of working out the meaning of unknown words and expressions from the context. The second is *Look Back*, which aims to help learners become familiar with the different ways of talking about the past in English by emphasising the meaning before the grammar.

As well as these two books, Hastings has written four non-fiction works on aspects of British and New Zealand history: *Over the Mountains of the Sea*, *Extra! Extra! How the people made the news*, *The Many Deaths of Mary Dobie* and *Odyssey of the Unknown Anzac*.

What the critics say

The Vocabulary Detective

In order to help the necessary learner training and development of the right attitudes, Hastings has written six stories which are fun to read, and which come with selected words or phrases highlighted in the text. The stories are followed by notes on these lexical items ... The stories are graded to some extent; they are aimed at C1/C2 levels ... but there are a lot of colloquial and idiomatic expressions, too. If you think that you would like to work with stories or texts pitched at higher or lower levels, you can do use different texts and just use the idea or the formula the author has created for dealing with lexical bumps in extensive reading activities.

Hanna Kryszewska, *Humanising Language Teaching*

He certainly writes with an element of realism. After each story, he extracts key vocabulary and suggests which questions and clues are most relevant to solve the lexical mystery. He also prepares readers for the fact they may not always solve the case. Sometimes the trail goes cold, sometimes you nab the wrong guy. However, he certainly gives all vocabulary detectives a

fighting chance as the level of detail in the scaffolding is impressive.
Meg Shovelton, *Modern English Teacher*

Over the Mountains of the Sea
The nautical experiences of these migrants ... are presented in absorbing detail in Hastings' book.
Kennedy Warne, *New Zealand Geographic*

Hastings ... has a journalist's eye for a good story and a historian's determination to work out what the stories mean.
Deborah Montgomerie, *New Zealand Books*

This is a very entertaining and user-friendly tale, or tales, written with a journalist's eye for the curious and bizarre as well as the broader detail.
Mick Ludden, *Wairarapa Times-Age*

Hastings ... demonstrates that the journey was even more stressful than we suspected, testing even for people used to a level of hardship that we have trouble imagining.
Gordon McLauchlan, *New Zealand Herald*

Extra! Extra! How the people made the news
This look at Auckland's early newspapers mixes entertaining anecdotes with bigger philosophies.
Kevin Childs, *The Walkley Magazine*

Extra! Extra! covers the turbulent fortunes of Auckland's newspapers over six decades, from the 1840s to the turn of the century .... the book gives an illuminating and well-rounded history of the papers, their place in the community and country and their unending efforts to attract and retain readers.
Michael Potts, *Media International Australia*

153

An excellent book that seamlessly combines scholarship with a feel for the dynamics of newsgathering and the reading public's insatiable curiosity about human frailty.

Ian F. Grant, *Journal of New Zealand Studies*, **2013**

The Many Deaths of Mary Dobie

This is not a thriller or a whodunnit: indeed it is meticulously researched, thoughtful, unshowy and compassionate. It is compulsive reading nonetheless.

William Brandt, *New Zealand Books*

It's a book that I, as a public historian, really find quite exciting …. A sophisticated retelling of New Zealand history, trying to understand what happened from different perspectives.

Paul Diamond, Radio New Zealand

Odyssey of the Unknown Anzac

Behind every name on the rows of headstones in New Zealand servicemen's cemeteries … is a story to be told. This is one such story, told by a writer whose lifetime in journalism ensures it has been told with attention to detail and great humanity.

Jim Sullivan, *Otago Daily Times*

A new and fascinating work of history …Hastings proceeds to reconstruct McQuay's war and journey to the mental hospital. This is not an easy task. There is no memoir, no letters, even the army record is deficient. Hastings manages to do so through a brilliant use of sources.

Jock Phillips, *New Zealand Review of Books*

Odyssey of the Unknown Anzac draws the reader's thoughts towards aspects of the war experience – post-traumatic stress, disability and mental illness – that sit awkwardly with commemorative myths of returned heroes and the glorious dead.

Samuel Finnemore, *New Zealand Listener*

Printed in Great Britain
by Amazon